The Sadness First Aid Kit

There's no panacea for sadness,
but there is a first aid kit.

Author: Phongmanus Budsayaprateep
Editor: Barbara J. Vincent
English translation: Sirirada Pattara-angkoon
Cover: Chanamon Roonsamrarn

Special thanks to Arpapond Ussanarassamee, Kratsanee Trakuntongchai, Rasa Salakij & Yuttana Roongthumskul

Preface

Sorrow or sufferings can affect anyone, regardless of whether they are male or female, old or young, filthy rich or dirt poor. It happens regardless of nationality and occupation. Everyone has experienced it.

At times, we encounter a minor woe that quickly vanishes and at other times, a great misery that is tremendously difficult to ignore. This suffering is something nobody wants, not a state anyone would wish for themselves. It is unlikely anyone would willingly plunge head-on into suffering. Humans have fought against it for centuries, attempting to mitigate, flee, or protect themselves from it.

For this reason, there exists a multitude of beliefs, ways of thinking, techniques, and other methods available to lessen suffering – or to allow the individual to experience immense happiness. The many systems of thought are often published in books. This type of text can often be found in the market irrespective of era. The book in your hand is another such book.

Many books aimed at combating suffering, the author finds, were typically written from the point of view of "someone who is happy looking at the perspective of those in suffering." This often made me feel as though there remains a considerable distance between the expectations of the writer of such books and the reader's current state, including the appropriate method of dealing with emotional issues which could require a huge change on the reader's part to implement. The path to self-help, thus, would seem even further off and more difficult to achieve.

Nevertheless, I'm not claiming those books are not effective in their way, but argues that there may be more fitting approaches that would work better for many individuals who suffer. When one is in such a state of suffering, strength and motivation may be lacking and looking towards a long-term goal may seem too unrealistically far off and impossible to achieve. In the end, individuals may give up altogether because they fear they will fail.

I wished to write a book that sees things from the perspective and situation of those in suffering as **"someone in the same boat"** and sought to find a **gradual form of progress, hand-in-hand with the reader** instead of talking from a perspective of someone who has succeeded that we have seen in countless other books. My goal is not to delve in too deep or to fully eradicate the root of suffering, but to simply deal with suffering in easy steps and assist in setting goals that appear plausible to do **at the moment** and that are not **out of reach**. Only when you feel an increase in motivation to move further and when the pain in your heart begins to heal, you will be ready to utilize other methods which may yield better results but be much more difficult to implement.

Even though humans can hardly remove all suffering from the world, it does not mean that the path to do so does not exist. Humans were designed to endure some suffering, irrespective of the cause. My hope is that we can get through these emotional struggles together.

I thank all who read this book of mine.

Phongmanus Budsayaprateep

Contents

Prologue **9**

Humans were Designed to Endure Suffering ...   15

Stopping Suffering is Difficult, but There
are Ways to Deal with It   20

Chapter 1: The Painful Past **29**

The Present is the Fruit of the Past.................   35

Past Experiences Always Have Value   41

The Past, Suffering, and Remembrance   50

Hold Firmly Onto Happiness........................   58

When Past Joy Becomes Present Sorrow   65

The Memory Suited for Healing   68

The Unchangeable Past is Not a Bad Thing   71

Chapter 2: The Long-Awaited Future **78**

What If It Turns Out Bad?   84

This, Too, Shall Pass   91

Planning Ahead for Potential Suffering   99

Let's Think of Something Else   105

Failing in the Past, as One May in the Future ...   111

There Are Two Sides to the Future Coin   114

The Future and Destiny 119

Chapter 3: The Present, the Body, and the Mind   125

The Tired Body Tires the Soul;
the Sick Body Sickens the Soul....................... 129

Force a Smile to Smile For Real 134

Do Nothing-Yet 138

Face It Together, Walk Away If Necessary 144

Search for Happy Memories 150

Don't Throw Everything Away 154

The Time Will Come When You're Ready 160

Rehearse in Writing 164

Talk about Your Suffering to Change
Your Thoughts 171

The Event, the Reasoning, and the Emotions 175

What We Want and What We Are Capable Of .. 182

Afterword 189

Prologue

"…The first time I realized I was an adult was when I discovered that suffering was present every single day.

Despite the individual differences in suffering, it is ever-present. We don't know when it will ever end. This is a fact that's hard to accept. When I think back to when I was much younger, I never had to experience such emotional pain. Life was easy. There was nothing to stress about, hurt my soul, or cause me suffering. In that way, I envy my past self.

I wondered why it is we experience suffering. What is this suffering thing, really? What are the benefits? What good does it do for someone to suffer? Does it do the world any good? Wouldn't it be nice if this thing called suffering could disappear from the world…?"

Greetings, Everyone

The book you're reading now will introduce you to the thing closest to you, the thing that is always by your side. Perhaps, you could even say it hardly ever leaves you. It is forever close by. Well…is there anything that would love us any more than it can? However, it is nothing that anyone would ever want near us. Because it is something known as:

"Suffering"

Have you ever noticed? No matter how little you want to encounter it, suffering has come to find you. Be it great, medium, or small in scale.

Suffering and happiness are things you don't have to learn from anyone. We innately come into this world knowing what happiness is and, conversely, what suffering is.

Suffering can happen at any age, even when we are very young. Childhood, the age many adults consider the most joyous time of our lives, can hold suffering. For example, being bullied by peers, scolded by teachers, or stressing over a test.

Adolescence is another time of suffering. The most obvious source of pain appears to be love and relationships. Many teens face emotional toils like heartbreak or the burden of riding the line between childhood and adulthood.

Emerging into adulthood is even worse. Work, finances, responsibilities, and other sources of stress can be easily listed without much effort.

Suffering comes to everyone. And despite its being commonplace, I doubt anyone would want to encounter it.

Everyone wants to be happy. We all want to destroy or escape suffering but, as previously mentioned, because it is never far away from us, new forms of suffering will always greet us.

When it is on a small scale, it's not hard to ignore or accept as part of the many colors of life. However, often, it may do more than simply color our lives. At times, the suffering can prove itself to be a big issue. If you have ever faced a major problem, you will likely understand what I'm talking about. Sometimes we drown in one source of suffering for an extended period--for months, a year, or for many years.

Suffering takes many shapes. It can come in the form of stress, worry, paranoia, fear, or many other negative emotions. Stress is one form that we face quite often. Some of us many even meet with it every working day.

Suffering is not something to look forward to nor is it something fun. Even to those who are experienced with suffering, it is remains an unwanted guest wherever they are.

It is stubborn and arrives without an invitation. So how can we find a way to deal with it?

Before we address that question, however, we must get to know it.

Regardless of how much we may want to run away, the path to overcoming something is as an age-old truism goes: "One who knows the enemy and knows himself will not be in danger in a hundred battles."[1] That is why we must first get to know suffering better before moving on.

This book will allow you to know more about both suffering and happiness. Not because it is always next to us, but in order to deal with it appropriately. The author has divided the contents into three main sections: **suffering caused by the past, suffering caused by the future**, and lastly the **connection**

---

[1] The Art of War by Sun Tzu

between body and mind; including how to deal with present suffering.

We can then see suffering in a clearer light and find ways to defeat its different forms.

But before getting into details, let's take a step back and get the bigger picture on suffering.

Humans were Designed to Endure Suffering

"Thou hast no sorrow in thy song, no winter in thy year."

John A. Logan –
Former American political leader and soldier

There is psychological research[2] that has found that humans are more responsive to negative than positive experiences. This makes us more receptive to pain and suffering when compared to happy things.

Have you noticed?

---

[2] Baumeister, R. F, et al. (2001). Bad is stronger than good. *Review of General Psychology, 5*, 323-370.

Going back to the question in the prologue that asks why we have to face suffering in this world. What benefits are there to it? Or is it a permanent fixture in human life?

In psychological theory, it is generally accepted that every emotion and feeling we experience has a cause.

Living organisms are designed to avoid harm. Suffering is a representation of things that can harm us. Thus, we are especially sensitive to suffering. Happiness is the converse. It comes with things that benefit us. We have suffering which signals us to avoid what is bad for us and happiness to tell us to chase after things that are good.

In ancient times, suffering for humans often meant starvation, predation, natural disasters, and physical pain. If we weren't adapted to be sensitive to suffering and take great measures to avoid it, humans would likely have been extinct a long time ago from an inability to avoid danger.

Despite the fact that present-day dangers are far fewer and less extreme than in the past, such as gaining a pound or two from stress-eating[3], the same mechanisms are still able to make us feel quite terrible.

---

[3] In truth, the situations leading to stress were usually linked to the evolutionary survival of most species in one way or the other. As such in the case of weight, despite having no real negative consequence on the individual, they still might worry that their loved ones might not be happy about it and plague us with the idea of not having a mate. This, in the end, comes back to the fear of inability to reproduce.

Thus, it's unsurprising if you have a lot of suffering and feel that life is a gray backdrop of unhappiness (we will cover this more in the next chapter) because this is in our nature.

Aside from having a significant effect on our lives, suffering can negatively impact our health as well. Many adults will understand how it leads to insomnia, gastritis, upset stomach, and much more.

On the converse, although it is true that happiness really does bring a whole lot of benefit to us, in contrast to suffering, the impact from happiness can't overcome the negative impact of suffering. Put in terms of points as measurement for the impact, an instance of suffering may be equivalent to 10 points while an instance of happiness might not even reach 5 points.

It might appear as if humans were made to feel suffering. Suffering also seems to endure inside us. Thus, suffering still exists even when we have all the improved techno-logy, well-developed religions, and scientific research to support healthy and happy living. The issue of suffering has traveled with us from the olden days of the human race until this very day.

However, even though we are creatures who are quick to feel suffering, it doesn't mean that we are incapable of dealing with it. If you're suffering too greatly at a given moment or wish to escape from a state of sorrow, stress, or worry, please don't despair. Because in the next chapter, we will be learning more about suffering in order to better deal with it.

But before that, I want to ask you: how much are you suffering at the moment?

Stopping Suffering is Difficult, but There are Ways to Deal with It

The question of how much is a lot in terms of suffering and how much is only a little is a hard question to answer.

Suffering has no real numerical scale like the units mentioned in the last chapter. It is not like temperature or the speed of a car that can tell us exactly how much is a lot and how much is a little. Suffering is internal. It's hard to tell how much one suffers.

Many times, we attempt to measure it in relation to the events that caused the suffering. If it's something quite intense, causing a lot of negative effects, or is a case of life-and-death, we often believe a lot of distress occurs. On the other hand, if the situation is on a smaller scale or had less of an impact on our lives, we tend to believe it causes little suffering.

If Dan failed a math test, he would feel more distressed than Arnold who failed to get a top score in his class.

If Natalie had influenza, she would suffer more than if she were to gain a pound.

If Phil was worried about important company business, he would feel worse than if he were worried about a coming first date.

If I were to have a big argument with my family, I would feel greater suffering than if my girlfriend didn't pick up my call.

But is each of these statements true?

In real life, we may discover that such generalizations are not always borne out. Have you ever found yourself stressing over something you thought wasn't that big an issue? Someone else in the same boat might also feel different about the same distressing situation. Some suffer a lot, others a little, and yet others still might have medium levels of suffering. Certain things may seem petty to us, but there are others who might not suffer at all even when they are buried deep in a stressful situation.

Because **we place importance on things differently**, some things we hold dear might not really have any effect on the lives of others. A student may give higher importance to going to all the movies instead of studying even when their grades may determine a huge part of their future. If something is important to us, we will suffer more over it than over things we don't consider so.

For example, Dan doesn't care much about his studies. He's used to failing. Flunking another test might not make him too happy, but he isn't likely to lament over it for more than half a day either. Not getting a top score for the first time in his life for Arnold, someone who has ranked first in class all his life, might be something he stresses over for months.

At times, similar situations may evoke differential suffering. If we had an argument with one friend, we might experience a lot of suffering. But if the same argument was with another friend we weren't as close to, we might not feel much of anything. Perhaps, even the same situation occurring at different times can result in different levels of suffering as well.

That is why it is difficult to quantify whether somebody suffers more or whether one occurrence can induce more suffering than another. It depends on our individual differences. Suffering is how we evaluate our experience. If we believe something will cause us a lot of suffering, that very belief might instigate or aggravate our suffering. How severely we evaluate the potential emotional pain is up us.

The only person to know how much you are suffering is yourself. If the person expresses their struggles, we might be able to take a guess at understanding, but if he or she keeps it to him or herself, it will be immensely difficult for others to know.

The reason I mention this topic first is because most people suffer and know they are suffering, but they refuse to acknowledge the fact and try to convince themselves that what is happening to them doesn't matter. They may try to tell themselves that worries like these are something only for the "immature," "people with a low EQ," or somehow **"defective."** This pressures them to force themselves to stop the suffering.

But hiding one's suffering doesn't really make it disappear, does it?

This is why, if you were to find yourself suffering, no matter how small the cause, I ask that you first learn to accept the fact that you are indeed suffering and refrain from seeing the suffering as some sort of "glitch" on your part. Because it is something natural that everyone experiences. We are not always rational in terms of our emotions.

Anyone can suffer. Whether the problem is large or tiny, how we can deal with it is an essential topic.

Some may view dwelling on things that have already happened or constantly reviewing a state of suffering already present in one's heart as the opposite of nipping an issue in the bud. And I would agree. There are other ways of solving the issue. For example, looking at the situation in a different light to avoid being emotionally affected is more likely to be effective. I believe it's an appropriate way of dealing with the issue, if it's possible.

Nonetheless, from my own experience and the stories as well as observations of those around me, I find that despite the efficacy of a solution that looks directly at the problem, it is often difficult and time-consuming to accomplish.

As I've said that suffering is how we evaluate our experience, thus refraining from evaluating our experiences may also result in a lack of suffering. If this is the case, is it really easy to command yourself "not to suffer"? If you could do that and succeed in lowering your suffering, it means you are able to change your way of thinking. I would congratulate you on that as it is one of the ways to be rid of suffering.

But from what I can see, **most people might think "This isn't something so serious that I should suffer over it, but still do."** Regardless of the fact that they understand the cause of their suffering is how they see things, they can't just switch off this process but continue to suffer.

Our feelings and emotions are inside of us. We can't physically observe what's going on. We can only infer what it is that we are feeling. Because we can't directly control our feelings, it's not possible for us to simply say to ourselves "Hey, why would I stress over something like this?" or "Actually I should feel happy in this situation. Okay, feel happy, feel happ--". It's usually not possible.

That's why I want to propose a different alternative. One I feel is easy to implement and uncomplicated for those in emotional pain. This approach doesn't focus on solving the problems at the root of our suffering and is more like fixing the surface issues, comparable to using first aid on a wound. To first stop the bleeding in our soul enough for us to recover some strength and move past the critical point.

If we are strong enough, we will have the strength to move on with our lives. Once we reach that point, we may be able to train ourselves in other methods of dealing with the problems.

But at the moment, let's deal with the surface issues. Let's clean and disinfect the wound before a worse infection eats into a bigger area of our soul--in simple steps.

Let's begin, starting with getting to know suffering better, like a new friend. This way, we will be better equipped to deal with it using **techniques you can employ here and now**. I guarantee it won't be so hard you feel hopeless and effective enough for you to walk forward to the next day. If you're ready, just turn to the next page.

Chapter 1: The Painful Past

"…Every day, when I open my eyes in the morning, my mind is still blank with drowsiness. But as soon as I come to my senses, the first thought that comes to mind is sadness.

Even though we broke up many months ago, the pain has stayed with me continuously. The thought that, if only I could turn back time, I would fix everything and make it better. If only I hadn't said that one thing, if I had done everything right, he would still be beside me. This thought made me suffer more than anything.

I can't imagine how much longer it will take for me to wake up and find myself no longer hurting from that.

I might have to be in this state until I die…"

The example situation above is clearly one of parting ways with a loved one.

If you, the reader, have been hurt by love at some time in your life, you will likely understand the story above. How much it hurts to be heartbroken and disappointed by love and how much suffering it can cause.

The issues concerning love may be considered the basic foundations for suffering in this world, regardless of the time or era. If you notice in novels or even in real life, for people close to you or for strangers, you will find that the cause of a lengthy sorrow is often love.

You probably have seen someone depressed and down for a long time because they were heartbroken, haven't you? Although it's true some people recover faster, within the span of a few weeks (particularly those with a new love interest), some may wallow in their sorrows for years.

With a lover's change of heart and their decision to walk away, some suffering occurs. However, when the love is still there but their significant other was taken away unexpectedly and permanently, the suffering one feels is even greater.

The pain of losing a lover is expressed in this quote from the comic, *The Embalmer*[4]:

When someone's child dies, the person loses their future.

When someone's friend dies, the person loses their past.

When someone's lover dies, the person loses the present.

The way I interpret this series of statements is that when a child dies, his or her parent loses hope. When someone loses a friend, it's as if the person loses the happy memories created with their friend. But if a

---

[4] Written and drawn by Mitsukazu Mihara

person loses his or her significant other, how then will they live with such loneliness in the present?

I've taken some time over this topic because I want to emphasize how every though a loss may occur in an instant, the suffering that results from that loss may remain for a very long time. Dumping someone may take only a few minutes, and waving goodbye may be the matter of a few seconds, but the suffering we feel stays with us for considerably longer. Still, long-term suffering doesn't arise from love alone. There are other, equally lengthy, causes of suffering.

You likely have heard the word "stigma": a sense of disgrace, both by the surrounding community and by the perpetrator himself, occasioned by past wrongdoing. It needn't be something very serious, but for example something like failing at an important job task might be enough to cause a sense of stigma among colleagues.

A single mistake in life can cause an individual to give up on goals, important opportunities, and more. Imagine an athlete who is just one second out of step and loses to a competitor in the final match. At a particular age, it might be the last chance they had to compete in such a high level match.

The things that continuously haunt us through a sense of stigma can also cause us suffering.

Past events influence the present and future for such a long time.

If suffering was only fleeting and vanished quickly, it wouldn't be so terrifying. But, in reality, it can stay with us for a long time and refuse to leave no matter what.

In this chapter, we will seek to understand more about suffering in terms of the things which have occurred in the past. The suffering stays despite the cause having already passed. We will be getting more familiar with this particular form of suffering in order to deal with it, beginning with problems, followed by solutions, and lastly we will conclude this chapter with the topic of suffering of the past once again.

The Present is the Fruit of the Past

If we were to look at the past as events that have passed, without the need to care or worry about them, it wouldn't cause us to suffer. But the past is not always completely in the past. It often can be the origin of current events as well.

A woman, after being cast aside by her lover, fails into a pit of depression every evening. Although it may be true that break-ups are painful, the thing that haunts her most is the fact that every evening she would spend time with the person who ate dinner, took nightly walks, watched movies with her, and drove her around. However there is no one to perform such tasks alongside her now. While it's true these tasks aren't in themselves difficult for her to perform, the difficulty lay in the loneliness these tasks now caused her to feel.

Parting ways is not something nice to experience. But the most pain can often come afterward. Present routines that have changed because of the unhappy event frequently cause suffering. Sometimes, **if the changes in our present didn't burden us so much, past events wouldn't be so overwhelming to us**

This stands as the major reason why, when one parts ways with a previous love and luckily finds another, that the suffering from the past will dissipate much more quickly. Because there is a replacement to lessen the blow of the impacts of the past on our present life (Regardless, I don't believe hurrying to find get into another relationship is the right solution. I believe that finding someone you will really love doesn't happen from effort but having the serendipity in meeting the right person. Forcing yourself to love someone may ease initial suffering but nothing good will come of it for the relationship in the future).

The same mentality functions with other issues, not just with love. Success is another great example.

An office worker feels terrible every time he walks past the office of his new department manager. The manager was a former colleague who used to be in the same position as he. But because our office worker had made a mistake in his work last month – and only due to that one mistake alone--it affected his promotional evaluation. He missed that chance to move up the corporate ladder, and his friend took the spot instead.

If that mistake was only dealt with by a reprimand from his supervisor and didn't result is such a tangible effect, it would seem as if nothing had changed. Suffering results from the things that have passed no too long ago. **But when we contrast our past with our present and further with our hopes for what**

could have been, we suffer every time we make that comparison.

Just as when we have a life-threatening illness that we learn can be remedied, if we discover that the strong pain or sadness we are experiencing will dissipate in the long run, then we are able to live our lives normally afterwards. A serious and painful illness from which we can recover in a short time may not seem so bad compared to a less serious illness with effects that will stay with us for many years or never be completely cured.

Aside from this, the past has major consequences in the present, **because we are unable to go back and change anything.**

The past is history. If we aren't allowed to travel back in time, we are rendered helpless to alter what has happened. Because the past is permanent.

A single outburst can cause lovers to part ways, lovers who will never have the chance to undo what has been done. Or an office worker who forgot his appointment with a client which causes the company a great loss. Similarly, the individual is unable to turn back time to meet his client.

We may feel it's a silly mistake that shouldn't have happened and lament on how, if only we could go back in time for a moment, everything would have been much better. But the problem is that we can't.

The what-if scenario we make up about how we would have been much happier is one of the reasons why we suffer over the past.

If I hadn't spoken that way, I wouldn't have argued with him. He would still be with me today.

If only I was more careful, I wouldn't have been in that accident that turned my life upside down.

The more we compare our lives with **"the present that doesn't exist"** the more we suffer.

How can we deal with the suffering that results from the past? How do we face the realities that can't be changed?

Past Experiences Always Have Value

"Forgiving does not erase the bitter past. A healed memory is not a deleted memory. Instead, forgiving what we cannot forget creates a new way to remember. We change the memory of our past into a hope for our future."

Lewis B. Smith – Ethicist and theologian

The first thing we should tell ourselves frequently is that **there exists no one in this world who has never made a mistake.** And I also believe that there is no one is this world who has not committed a serious blunder. The word serious doesn't always have to equate to something as terrible as causing the death of someone else, losing a fortune, or becoming physically disabled. But

I believe that after we all have grown into full-fledged adults, sooner or later we will encounter situations where we make mistakes, mistakes that cause us great suffering. If there are people who have not encountered such situations, they are extremely fortunate. How-ever, the type of mistakes are up to the individual. The same mistake that seems to be serious in one person might not seem so serious to others.

Thus, there is nothing unusual about making mistakes. This is something everyone has encountered in some shape or form. At this stage, I ask nothing other than that you try to side with your past self as much as possible.

Humans often have a questions about their past. Why did they do or fail to do a certain thing in the past? In hindsight, it appears so simple what the right choice should have been. So why did you choose the wrong path? In reality, however, we only think that way because the situation is in the past. We now have the added insight of knowing what our choice would come to and can guess at what the better choice might have been. Our past self never had that kind of privilege because he or she lacked the information that comes with experience. **We can't use our present, knowing self as some sort of standard against which we measure our past self. It's simply not logical.**

In this regard, the next thing we have to do in order to lessen our own suffering is to **stop blaming our past selves.** We acted the way we did because we had no way of predicting the results of our actions. If we had known, there was no way we would have done the things we did.

We have to take responsibility for our past errors. We have suffered greatly from them. You could say that we have made a mistake and have already received punishment for that mistake. It is now time for us to forgive ourselves.

At the very least, when we don't pressure or criticize ourselves so much, it lessens our suffering.

And what of the consequences of those mistakes? How should we deal with them?

I believe the negative consequences of the past are alterable. If you who are suffering are able to rectify the situation in the present – for example, attempting to go back to a former lover– it's likely that you've already tried to do so. If a person could repair a mistake made at work, they probably have already tried. But there are certain things they can't be changed. There are certain things that have already occurred and are irreversible. In that case, we can't go back to change what has happened. We can only accept it as it is.

Nevertheless, as I have mentioned previously, everyone has done something wrong.

But the results of that mistake don't necessarily have to be entirely negative.

Errors of the past--if they aren't serious enough to kill us—can become a valuable lesson, a point of comparison for our unknowing self. Because such errors at least **allow us to know what we shouldn't do in the future.**

Regardless, if we are still living and breathing, such lessons have the potential to benefit us in the future. Our struggles with that lesson will not be for nothing.

The important thing to remember is that, in a sense, we can always change the past. But not the past that has come and gone. Rather, it's the here and now that we can act on. **Because the present is the past of the future.**

If we have made errors because we did things we now believe to be inadequate or contrary to our well-being, what we should do now is to do our best. Even without knowing the results of our present actions, if nothing else **we will have fewer regrets because we have done our very best.**

If we did something wrong because we chose an incorrect path, we can look to the past and know that we won't make the same mistakes again.

The more hurt we are, the deeper the scar. But scars like this help us remember and prevent us from making the same mistake twice.

This is why, even though we have made mistakes, there are benefits. It is like when we have walked the wrong path and failed to find what it is we were looking for, that doesn't mean we have achieved nothing. But although the benefits of our mistakes aren't immediately apparent, they may yield benefits in the future.

In my opinion, when we feel sorrow about past events, it's a form of **"taking responsibility."** Past mistakes make us feel sad or hurt because we know the value of what we lost due to those mistakes.

When we are feeling sad about losing a loved one, it is because the person is important to us.

When we are tormented because of a mistake that caused us to lose an opportunity, it is because we have dream, aspirations we aim for, goals we don't want to miss out on or postpone.

A person who loses something they hold dear but feels no pain or regret would not be considered a normal human being. Perhaps, they may already have achieved enlightenment or maybe they have been completely detached from the feelings and emotions that plague the typical person. Or alternatively, it could be that the things they lost weren't really of much importance to them.

Sadness is, then, something normal which is one expression of the value we place on particular things, events, or people when some such thing is lost forever, it's natural to feel sadness.

So feel free to be sad. It's not something out of the ordinary.

However, don't forget. We are not merely living for the present. This very second we're breathing; we can't guarantee how much longer we have to live. But we still have the near future, and the far.

If we were to feel misery or regret about what has happened in the past, if we keep clinging to the idea that if we could turn back time, we could do so much better… But we all know we can't do anything to the past because there's no way to turn back time. This is why, instead of lamenting over how we could've fixed the past or eradicated events from the past that affect our present, we should train ourselves to fix the future.

As for our present sadness, we should let it live with us, but we can't allow it to dim down our future. If the sadness doesn't cause us to engage in self-blaming or self-hatred, it's possible to live with it for a while.

Of course, long-term exposure to sadness isn't a good thing. Even those who see suffering as a feeling of responsibility for the things we consider valuable know that we shouldn't wallow too deeply or too long in sorrow. As our next topic, we shall familiarize ourselves with sadness about the past and how to deal with it.

The Past, Suffering, and Remembrance

As previously mentioned, if suffering is merely fleeting, whether big or small in scale, it won't be too much of a problem. However the suffering that hangs onto us is greatly troublesome indeed.

If a typical person tries to imagine the bad occurrences of the past, they may find that they are able to recall many such events. But if they were to try to imagine the good things that have happened, instead, they may find it much harder. Perhaps, only a few fleeting memories may pop up.

Troublesome events are recalled with greater ease, and we are often able to clearly think back to the things that took an emotional toll on us. Because it is in our nature, we suffer from the bad things of the past for a very long time.

The present and the past are connected by memory. We have talked about how, despite the past being gone, it can still cause us suffering. One reason for this is because the past has negative consequences in the present. However, not all suffering over the past has such a direct cause. The simple action of thinking back to negative events of the past is enough to make us suffer, even in the absence of current negative consequences.

If we argued with a friend, for example, or had a loved one speak harshly to us or tease us about our flaws; despite there not being any consequences or direct effect in the present, just thinking about the anger or sadness that result from that situation is enough to make us suffer.

And why is that so? Why do the negative events stick so well in our minds? Similarly, we are more likely to think about negative situations than positive ones.

If we were to search for the answer to the question of differential memory, we would have to look back to the start of where we remembered the memory. Humans are very biased. **We care more for the bad things than the good ones.** The things that make us feel good, we may remember fleetingly. However, the things that cause us to feel terrible we pay a lot more attention to it.

Try to think back to your past. When you encountered a situation that made you angry or sad, do those situations disappear from your memory in a heartbeat or do they linger on?

Try to imagine if you were to find a twenty-dollar bill on the floor. How happy does that make you feel?

What if the scenario is different? If you were about to take a bill from your purse and suddenly a gust of wind caused the note to slip from your hands. Blown away into the road, the money is now lost. How would you feel about the situation?

Or…

If you received tremendous compliments from your boss, how many hours or days would your happiness last?

But if you were to get harshly reprimanded by your boss, how great would your suffering be?

When we experience something that makes us happy, we won't really think about the situation. We don't question the reason we are feeling happy or why happiness decided to knock on our door. But when it comes to suffering, we do care. We may search over and over for the reason why we suffering. If it was something serious, we may even lament about why it happened to us.

When someone gives us compliments, we curtly think it's because we did well. We are happy and feel good about ourselves. But if we were scolded, we would wonder in detail about why it was so. Did we do something wrong? Have we forgotten something? Or maybe it has nothing to do with our work. Perhaps, that very person simply has something against us. Will this have negative consequences? How should we react?

When such events occur, we can get badly shaken. We will become more vigilant, not allowing the little details to slip past. Thus, it causes us to get even more emotional and these intensified emotions burn the memory of the event more deeply into our minds.

As when we recite the Gettysburg address or the multiplication table, the more we think about it, the more invested we are, and the better we can remember.

Think again about the questions above: comparing your recall of negative events to your memory of positive ones, you may find that negative ones stay sharper in your memory, and you feel more deeply about them.

Moreover, thinking of past sufferings can serve as a foundation for further suffering in the present as well. This is how happenings in the past have the power to hurt our present.

A common example is when people argue. In the heat of the moment, it's difficult to recall the good things the other person did for us in the past. On the other hand, memories of the bad things can come pouring in. The more you think about it, the worse you feel about the person. The worse you feel, the angrier you get and the worse the conflict.

In another example, if someone who is in despair were to try to sit and think about the nice things that had happened to them, it would be very difficult. Negative thoughts are much easier to recall and can often cause a person in despair to feel even worse.

This state of being is typical of human nature. As we have touched upon previously, the things that cause us suffering are danger signals. Because of this status of "danger signal," we have evolved to be particularly sensitive to suffering when compared to happiness. Looking back to the time when human beings first roamed the earth, not receiving a certain reward could mean we had missed a good opportunity, but not being able to sense danger could cost you your life. Though society has developed and become more complex and in many ways safer, we are still those human beings who evolved to adapt to that long-ago world.

Regardless, humans have lived in a sophisticated social environment for some while now. Our present sufferings don't always pose danger. By knowing that we are sensitive to suffering by nature presents a strong foundation for understanding our-selves better. When we suffer, we can know it isn't always a true reflection of our current status.

But knowing our nature well isn't enough to mitigate suffering. So what should we do with the suffering of the past that reside in our memories?

Hold Firmly Onto Happiness

"We can only be said to be alive in those moments when our hearts are conscious of our treasures."

Thornton Wilder – American writer

It's painstakingly hard to stop ourselves from remembering and reminiscing about past suffering. Due to the deep mechanisms of our being, it's as if we were programmed since birth to be this way. However, we can make our happiness clearer in our memories and easier to remember.

Even when happiness and suffering are such different feelings, they still compete for the same space in our memories. If we retain a lot of bad memories and fewer happy ones, we will be less happy. But if we had the same amount of terrible memories and good ones, we will be much better off.

Happiness is something considerably fortunate. It's what everyone seeks. But when it visits, we are only able to enjoy it fleetingly. And, in a blink of an eye, **we forget and let it fall into the past.** Some moments of happiness don't even leave a trace in our memory.

Thus, if we want our happiness to not disappear like a mere vapor but to stay and fill our thoughts, we ourselves must grasp onto these moments of happiness.

Think about when most people talk to their close relations. The main topics of conversation tend to be looking for commiseration over bad experiences. We may only touch on these topics, and it's quite easy to bring them up. This is normal and only natural. But we are less likely to talk about our happiness.

Moreover, in many societies, telling people of all the happiness we encounter might not be appropriate for every setting. Although many would be open to listen and share our joy, some would interpret it as bragging and not be as willing to lend an ear. Still if we're sure the person in question enjoys listening to our stories of happiness, doing so may increase our happiness. But even if we can't share our happy moments with others very often, we only have to **try and think often about these positive occurrences**, look at them in detail in the same way we look at our suffering.

Don't disregard even the smallest sources of joy and think that they're insignificant, not worthy of thinking about or celebrating. No matter if it was getting to have a favorite meal at dinner, achieving a new high score in a phone game, meeting an old friend you haven't seen in a long time, or experiencing less traffic than usual; we are often regrettably dismissive of the little things in life.

In truth, happiness, just like sorrow and suffering, will become merely an emotion if we put no thought into it.

It's understandably difficult not ruminating about things that cause us suffering. We frequently overthink small things that make us feel bad. Imagine if we had a dinner we didn't like, got a low score in a game, had somebody tell us that an acquaintance doesn't really like us, or had more traffic than usual. If we were to encounter these types of situation, it can cause us suffering in the present as we think over many small situations and pile them into one huge issue.

If we can't simply force these negative events from our mind, it would be much easier to give more attention to the good things that have happened. If we were to focus more on our happiness, those happy events would take up more space in our mind, even if negativity fills the majority of our thoughts. Even this little bit will make us feel happier.

Sometimes, caring more about our happiness will require us to make it more tangible with a physical reminder of some kind.

The mechanisms of our thoughts are invisible to us. One day, a negative event from the past might pop up out of the blue and cause us present suffering. It may be extremely difficult to put those thoughts aside and equally hard, if not harder, to tell ourselves to think positive thoughts.

But we can have a little help along the way. One kind of help comes in the form of **journaling** which can make our happiness more obvious to us.

If we encounter something that made us happy, instead of letting it pass us by, we should write it down either in a journal or put in down into words somewhere. Even if you don't have time to come back and read what you have written, this is not the main value of this process. When you're in the process of putting your experiences into words you are **more likely to give it more thought then you normally would** and you will feel more of its effect emotionally than you would if you were to give it no more thought.

The small, joyful events which we wouldn't typically pay much attention to, if we were to write them down and have them physically there in front of us, we might go from feeling as if there are no happy moments to realizing that they do occur. In the spur of the moment when we think that our lives are full of bad things, this journal will allow us to better recall the good events that have happened to us.

As an analogy, think of a small happiness as a delicious drink: it can make the less-than-enjoyable meal we are having easier to swallow. Like the popular lyric in the famous movie

Mary Poppins, "A spoonful of sugar helps the medicine go down." The one positive thing will give us more strength to deal with negativities we encounter.

And this is even truer if we experience something that brings us great joy. Writing such events down on paper would amplify the feelings, emotions, and thoughts and allow us to experience them for an even longer period than would ordinarily be the case.

When Past Joy Becomes Present Sorrow

"There is no greater sorrow than to recall happiness in times of misery."

Dante Alighieri – Middle Age Italian statesman,
poet and linguist

Sometimes past happiness won't provide us with happiness in the present. On the contrary, it may be the fuse for suffering and sorrow because there are **times when past happiness will turn into a point of comparison with the present which seems dim and not as joyful as before.**

In the previous chapter, I spoke about how we should hold onto happiness, in order to fill our memories with good thoughts and prevents ourselves from dwelling on negative memories and thus transforming past suffering into a present suffering.

However, some of you may wonder if it really works. You may wonder why, at times, the past joyful memories can cause such pain in your hearts.

If someone recently suffering a heartbreak were to recall the happy times with their ex, this would likely cause them a lot of pain. The feeling of "no longer having them with you" or "I'll never be that happy again" will make them feel even more pain instead of happiness.

If someone who previously held a prestigious position were to be demoted to a lower rank or were to retire, they might feel a sense of yearning. They may yearn for the time when many looked up to them, when they were a focus of respect. Wherever they went, people would be courteous. Whatever they did, people were sure to follow along.

Compared to those times, perhaps they would feel sorrowful about their current state which appears less satisfying.

If happiness is like "a treasure" that gives us satisfaction, the more we collect it and the more valuable it is, the question remains: how can it make us feel even more pain?

So what should we do in this situation? How do we stop our happiness from hurting us? How can we make it so that the past joy comes back to comfort us in times of need instead?

The Memory Suited for Healing

If we observe carefully, we will discover that past happiness that causes us suffering is usually a case of comparing a seemingly picture-perfect event with the present that might not be that great.

If we're freshly broken-hearted or have been dumped, the memories that cause us the most pain would be the loving recollections of our former lover. On the other hand, happiness from other aspects of our lives, for example: familial love, happy memories with our friends, or the elation from a great work achievement won't cause us more pain in this scenario.

If we're sad because we were demoted at work, the memories that cause the most pain might be memories of receiving a high promotion or of enjoying the respect of our colleagues. However, the happiness from other areas of life, like family or winning a sporting event wouldn't cause us that same pain.

Because when we recall happy times unrelated to our loss, we don't compare that past with our current state. Without comparing what we used to have and what we dearly long for, the pain will not be magnified. This is because the idea of losing something we used to have, and that we now want, will **increase the feelings of regret and wanting to have it once again** (despite knowing that it's impossible) and this will worsen our suffering even more.

However, the happy memories that don't cause us to make comparisons with our current state will reassure us that happiness is still with us. The more we think about them, the more satisfied we feel because such things brought us happiness in the past and are still going well (even if we don't feel quite as much joy about them, they're still something good in our lives).

We may have great suffering in one aspect of our lives, but having happiness in other parts of life will help **keep us afloat emotionally**. Thus, when we are wallowing in sorrow, we should try to find happy memories in other aspects of life to uplift our moods.

But as mentioned, happy memories are prone to being forgotten. Unlike the sad or troubling memories which stick to us, we have to practice paying attention to the good things and rehearse them over in our head.

Aside from that, forcing ourselves to think only of the good things and not of the bad ones isn't easy. Memories aren't just objects inside our heads. We can't always manipulate them the way we want. But at the same time, there are ways we can manage our memories. These techniques will be touched upon in the third chapter.

The Unchangeable Past is Not a Bad Thing

If we could turn back time, this book probably would not have been written. Because, in the end, the future would consists of us going back in order to rewrite our past the way we want it.

If we fought with a lover and said something out of the heat of the moment which ultimately resulted in a breakup, it's likely we would go back to right our mistake. And currently, our lover would still be with us.

If we made some sort of mistake at work that resulted in a poorly done project, we could go back to fix it. Then at present, our reputation would be intact, and we'd be set for future progress.

However, in my opinion, if time-travel was really possible and we were really able to go back in time, our lives would merely consist of going back into the past to fix our mistakes. Our present lives would cease to exist. Even our future would have no meaning. We would likely be reduced to obsessed people, wanting the past to be picture-perfect. I can't even begin to imagine how many times we each would travel back before we were truly satisfied with our past. It would become an endless loop that would prevent us from moving forward.

Regardless, at this point humans aren't able to travel back in time. We can't change what has happened. Thus, it's pointless to ruminate about how you would change your actions if only you could travel back in time.

This inability can be, in fact, a blessing in disguise. In truth, you can even call it one of the good things in life because it frees us from the burden of having to fix our past constantly.

Even though the faults of the past have a cost that carries over to the present, we are still able to lessen the blow--for example, if we made a mistake in our work and have to redo some work in order to fix it, we should do exactly that--this means that the "past issue" isn't really in the past. It's still occurring within the present. It's something we can still put our best effort into so that our future won't be as affected and so that we won't have to feel regret or ruminate about it in the future.

However, if that mistake still presents an effect in our current lives that we are unable to control--for example, if we accidentally broke a valuable vase--it doesn't matter how much regret we feel or how hard we try to fix it, because it will never be the same again. This inability to undo something in the past creates feelings of responsibility.

Such events leave us feeling bad, but without any requirement for further action.

Limit how much sadness you experience for something lost and don't allow yourself to be swallowed by it, **because it's the truth that you can't do anything about it.**

As I've mentioned, sadness isn't without its benefit. It serves as a lesson and a reminder that we can take with us into the future.

Even so, it doesn't mean that once we make a single mistake, we won't ever commit the same error again. The world doesn't operate that smoothly. That mistake can have multiple causes. The thing we can be sure of, however, is the fact that we learn and achieve growth every day from such mistakes. **Thus, our experiences are always valuable.**

As for the topic of sadness, if we have to wallow in the suffering of past days, we don't have to believe we'll be stuck that way until we die.

Humans have this magical gift known as **"forgetting."** Despite how bad things might get at times, our ability to forget allows the suffering to slowly fade away.

Even if it's true that our human nature is made so that we remember painful events so clearly and with such ease, no matter what type of memory it may be, it can be forgotten over time.

We don't just forget the contents. Our emotions pertaining to those memories will also fade as we remember it less clearly. You can try to observe an event that evoked unpleasant suffering. You may notice that the more time passes, the less effect that memory has on your emotional response. Think back to an event in your childhood which, at the time, seemed like the end of the world (if you ever experienced such a situation). Analyze your feelings in the present moment. Do you still suffer as intensely as you used to? Does the negative emotion still resound as strongly as ever? It's likely that the suffering has lessened in its intensity.

Time is a good friend to change. Both changes we wish for and those we don't. Changes transform us into something different. The person we were yesterday might be different from who we are today. **Humans are incredibly good at adapting, more so than we ourselves realize.** If despite all efforts we still feel that the suffering will haunt us and cause us pain for all of eternity, what we should do to counteract that is to wait. Today might simply not be the day.

When the day comes, you might not even realize that the suffering has evaporated along with the passage of time. It may not disappear completely, if it was something extremely serious and important to our lives. The sorrow might leave a scar. However that scar gradually heals until one day, we can't really remember what it was that caused that mark and that much pain.

We can't go back to fix the past, but we can let it dissolve with time. This is how things that are past and gone take care of themselves. Our job is to make the best out of the present so that it won't become the past we will regret in the future.

In this section, we mentioned how to deal with sufferings from the past. But we suffer from another dimension of time that is known as the future. We shall get to know and learn ways to deal with this cause of suffering in the next chapter.

Chapter 2: The Long-Awaited Future

"...Sitting is stifling. Staying still is impossible. Thoughts about my work keep circling in my head, so much that I have to get up and walk. But walking didn't help. My walks were circular just like my thoughts.

What if my project doesn't turn out well? What if my boss doesn't like it? How will it impact my salary? I heard that there was a team that failed and a few days after that, the team leader resigned. How will I fare then? That team leader was much more capable than I am...

The previous times my work hasn't turned out that well, despite my trying so hard. So what about this time? Will I actually survive this? I wish the presentation day would come quickly. But it's not until next month.

I don't want to worry anymore. I tried to tell myself to worry only a little bit, since it's futile anyway. But I can't help it. If I make a mistake, things will be very bad..."

Nothing is worse than things that have yet to occur.

Our sufferings, aside from being caused by past events, can have another cause which is future events.

We have this feeling called "anxiety." Anxiety can be considered a close relative to fear. However, they have their differences. Fear often arises from bad things that **definitely will happen** or have happened to us. For example, if we encounter a poisonous spider, have a quiz we have no idea about, or run into someone who has hurt us before, we will feel fear because we know that we might get hurt, be thrown into hardship, or be in danger.

But with anxiety, the things we are afraid of aren't in front of us but only exist as a possibility in the future. As of now, nothing has occurred. However, there are chances that we **might** have a quiz that we haven't studied or prepared enough for. We **may** have to face embarrassment from a work presentation. Another important point is **that even though it may or may not even happen to us** for certain, this worry can still manifest as anxiety.

If we were to compare, the past suffering will be like a scar of suffering that didn't heal properly. Like if we were to be burnt by a fire or slashed by a knife and have a wound that still hurts and leaves a mark. Thus, we still have sufferings in the present because it makes sense to be affected by things that have already occurred.

But if it were the case that we have never been burned or slashed by a knife previously, our anxiety has already hurt us. Our suffering would have been caused by something that has never existed. Once you think of it that way, suffering about the future may seem strange. If it hasn't happened yet, how does it affect us?

Humans are creatures with the most developed brain out of all animals. We are able to engage in foresight into the far future. But the one thing that comes with that amazing ability is an imagination that can cause bad feelings about events that haven't happened and that might not ever happen. Additionally, when those fears actually come true, the event might cause less stress than we are currently having.

However, this doesn't mean sufferings with a future cause are unusual, strange, or wrong. Everyone is, more or less, plagued by anxieties in their life.

The people who have moderate level anxiety might only encounter suffering and stress in their future that greatly impacts their life as it goes on. But those with chronic anxieties will always feel negative about things that might cause them suffering.

As with the previous chapter, we will discuss the nature of each type of suffering and the ways in which we can deal with them. This chapter closes with the summary of future sufferings.

It might sound strange, but we can "hold out against events that have not happened" together.

What If It Turns Out Bad?

"The future influences the present just as much as the past."

Friedrich Nietzsche – German Philosopher

Anxieties caused by the future are in part due to the fact that we know there is a risk inherent in a given situation. There are chances of failure, mistakes, or just encountering things that are unpleasant. What if we were to be unlucky or faced some bad result of our own actions? What should we do in that case? Can we deal with that if it happens? If we can't deal with it, can we survive that situation?

Imagine final exams week. The more importance those tests have for our lives, the more we worry. Final exams week for high school students can be considered a time in their lives where many suffer from the greatest level of worry. Most are anxious and worry that they might not be able to do well on the test. What if the things they have studied for and the contents of the test were different? What should they do if they get a low score or don't get accepted into their university of choice? If they have to take a gap year because they failed their test, how much will this affect their life?

One other example would be the imaginary scenario at the beginning of this section. It involves an office worker who worries so much about an important presentation that he can't sit still. He worries that his boss might not like his work and the consequences that would follow, and keeps on lamenting about what he would do if that actually happened.

Everyone has their "fated" day or event in the future that has the power to change their lives for better or for worse. Students have their exam times. Adults have important projects. Teenagers have their first dates. Mothers have the expected birth of a child. Patients have the day of their surgery. Because in this world both success and failure are possible, we can't help but think about what would happen if we fail. What would I do if I failed the test? What if I made an error in my work? What if she rejects my feelings, how would I continue to live on? Or if the birth doesn't go well, how will I deal with this? If the disease can't be cured, what will become of me?

You may realize that most things we are worried about often have two possible outcomes: the one we desire and the one we don't. However, as soon as we start to ruminate about it, we are less likely to imagine the outcome we want to see because our thoughts are clouded by the negative possibilities.

No matter the type of situation, the things we fear are often relatively rare. If we were to gather the statistics regarding these events (final test results, birth outcomes, etc.), the likelihood of our worst fears coming true would be low, but due to the power of worry, we are still afraid.

A frequent example is someone with a fear of flying despite knowing that the probability of a crash is extremely low--in fact, much lower than that of a deadly car accident. However, because the ultimate consequence of that event is so frightening, many people still have that fear when they board a plane. Most people are afraid of snakes but not mosquitos, even though snakes normally would escape from you rather than try to bite you, and malaria or other blood-borne diseases from mosquitos which bite you without hesitation are deadly. We humans are often anxious about things that are very unlikely to occur.

As another everyday life example, a student who has never failed a test and has always got good grades, might have anxiety over a certain test. If you had friends who are good at their studies who tell you after an exam that they did terribly and weren't sure of many questions, it's probably not because they intended to lie, but that this really was what they felt because they knew that they weren't a 100 percent sure about many of their answers, and their uncertainty amplified their anxiety.

Aside from thinking that the future might not turn out the way we wanted, **we fear much more serious consequences than actually occur when all is said and done.**

Someone who has to do a presentation for their boss might worry whether the latter would be displeased with their work. Will their salary be cut back? Will they get fired? Get passed by for promotion? Perhaps, in the case of a student, he or she might worry about whether they will worry about whether they'll get into college if they fail a test.

In truth, even if things don't go the way we expected, the results might not be as bad as we originally thought. As I already mentioned at the start of this section **there's nothing as bad as things that have yet to occur.**

If we observe carefully, we might discover many anxieties that often arise from our thinking and from our own fear that we might not be able to deal with whatever comes our way. We might encounter an unimaginably horrible thing or consequence that will follow us. How would we deal with it?

While it's true that "lowering expectations" can be a good thing, because when we allow room for disappointment, reality won't be as crushing. However, if anticipating failure causes us to suffer before the event as well as after consequences arrive, we leave ourselves open to suffering that is multiplied several times over.

How can we deal with suffering caused by this?

This, Too, Shall Pass

Although it's true that we worry because things may not turn out the way we want them to, if things turn bad and cause us problems and struggles, it's all part of how life goes.

While there are "chances" of a really bad possible outcome, the probabilities of such an outcome are usually quite slim.

Adjusting our thoughts to envision more of the positive outcomes may be beneficial. If we sit around weighing the possibilities of positive versus negative results, **many times we will realize that the possibilities of negative outcomes are extremely small.** It's as if we're tossing a die three times and worrying that it will always come up as "one," (with a probability of 1 in 216 throws).

Even if the probabilities of bad things happening in this world aren't as small as a throw of the dice, if we look at things objectively, we will see that as long as we come prepared there is little chance things will go wrong.

For example, a student who always attends class and reads their book before the exam may be anxious about failing a test but chances are that's very unlikely.

Nonetheless, changing one's thinking in a certain direction is not that easy. If we still feel in our hearts that "there's a chance things might go wrong," the anxiety will still plague us.

I have another way of thinking: **if the result was the worst possible outcome, will I still be able to deal with it?**

Consider all of the possible negative outcomes of making a mistake in our work: receiving a salary deduction or even getting fired (which, in reality, unless it's a really huge mistake, is highly unlikely). How would we deal with this situation? Is it really equivalent to losing your life or failing in life in general?

Getting a salary deduction or not receiving a raise is not a good thing. But if you think about it, you are still able to live as normal. As for getting fired, the chances are quite small. If we were to consider the worst of things with some degree of reason, the outcome may be that the company asks you to leave but according to labor laws, they would still need to pay you some type of compensation. This means we still have some time to look for a job. Obviously, that won't be easy, but it's not a death sentence either so we can still recover from it.

If we look at the worst possible outcome and find out that, at the very least, "we won't die" from it, it can ease our anxieties somewhat.

And truth be told, the chances of negative events like those are very small. The future events aren't usually so black-and-white. There will always be silver linings in dark clouds, most often ones we never anticipated.

With most life situations, it's not as if we can only get either a passing or a failing score on our tests.

Our boss might not especially like the work we did, but it's unlikely he would absolutely abhor the presentation we made. He might just consider it "all right" and not think much afterwards.

A surgery might not go extraordinarily well but the little side effects might only cause us to take a bit more time recovering.

If we were to look at things statistically, there's much more chance an event will come out in some in-between, gray area rather than either black or white. Regardless, as we mentioned previously, by nature humans tend to remember negative events better. Thus, we may trust our own memories too much because we are less likely to remember the positives or the neutral events and remember only the negatives.

Thus, you can emphasize to yourself the chances of getting lucky and getting everything the way you want it or being a little less lucky and having events not turning out the way you wanted but not too bad either. Or, you can be slightly unlucky, having to deal with some things that cause you to suffer a little. Or you might be unbelievably unlucky with nothing going your way.

Even if things were to go completely awry, you might not be happy but at the same time you might be able to deal with what has happened.

I want you to know one thing. Even if the situation turns out really badly, humans are still capable of coping. Truly, in this world, there are very few events we can't handle and regardless of who it is, we are all able to problem-solve and find a way out.

When we worry over how we would deal with the negative events or mistakes in the future, know **that we are more capable than we think we are.**

We may not be able to deal with the problem completely, but we can lessen the hardship.

Many may wonder if we should have a plan B just in case.

If we really can prepare for the outcomes we are afraid of, we should spend our time making that type of preparation instead of figuring out how to undo something. To illustrate, if we worry about the results of a test, we can study more rather than apply for a retake test. If we worry about work, we should put more of our effort in improving our future work instead of trying to fix a bad project.

Having a plan B is never a bad thing. But if I were to advise you, you should devise a back-up plan only when:

1) The mistake is something you can actually correct yourself. For example, you can prepare additional points for your presentation if your boss doesn't like your ideas. This is considered good preparation. But in the case of a surgery, you might not need to have a plan B because it isn't something you can control.

2) Having a plan B helps you relax. Irrespective of how useless the plan may be, if it allows you breathing room, you can do it. But if sitting around and planning for it worsens your anxiety, it might be better not to think too much about it. (We will talk about this topic in the following chapter.)

Sometimes, when we aren't facing problems head-on, we can't really see any clear solutions. Even if we don't believe in our own abilities, as I have said and emphasized before, humans are more capable of dealing with problems than we believe. We might not be able to deal with everything that happens but, in those cases, we usually can live with it. And the life-or-death events are few and far between.

Another thing is that, if we know ahead of time that something might go wrong, we are more likely to be better at dealing with it compared to things we never thought about before. It's analogous to driving: if you can see that the road ahead is very uneven, that is better than driving and suddenly feeling your car's front end drop into a pothole.

Thus, don't worry so much because this too shall pass. Think about it this way over and over until the worry about the future lessens.

Planning Ahead for Potential Suffering

"What else does anxiety about the future bring you but sorrow upon sorrow?"

Thomas à Becket – Archbishop of Canterbury d.1170

Humans are planners. We don't just live on a day-to-day or hour-to-hour basis.

When we're working, we might think about what we will have for lunch or what we should do after we clock out. What should we do this holiday? Should we take a vacation soon? We are planners who think of both the far and near future, by the hour, day, month, or even year.

It's normal to hope and dream about future happiness. Regardless of how the present is, being able to imagine the good things waiting for us in the future can make us very happy.

If we are students or office workers, there's nothing that makes us happier than a Friday evening. Knowing that you'll get two full days of rest is a pleasant feeling. That moment before the weekend might even be happier than the two weekend days because of the anticipation.

Our happiest times are when we are about to achieve happiness, not during the times we believe we are happy. To illustrate, it's like when we are buying something. We are happiest when we are about to purchase something we have always wanted or in the act of shopping. But as soon as we obtain those things, the happiness bar lowers dramatically (this may explain why people get addicted to shopping, even if they already have many possessions).

Thinking about future happiness can be considered as a plus. It's as if we get to experience the happiness beforehand even without having to invest time, money or energy. However, it is by this very same mechanism that you can experience suffering before it has even happened.

In the previous section, we talked about the uncertainty of the future. There's no sure-fire way of knowing what will happen, and once we start wondering whether things will go our way, we begin to feel anxiety and suffering in the present.

If we think about our future suffering, it's likely that we will also be suffering in the present.

If we speculate about the future and think ahead to an event that will likely turn out great, we will feel joyous ahead of time. On the other hand, if we imagine that it will turn out badly, we'll feel anxious over it. The more of a worrier you are, the more likely it is you will imagine something bad happening and suffer during the present.

Think of a child waiting in the principal's office for a punishment, or when his or her mother says "Wait here, I'm getting a stick to spank you with," or even when our boss says "Tomorrow will be very busy, so you can't take time off." We haven't been punished, spanked, or faced that mound of work yet, but we can already feel the stress beforehand.

Moreover, aside from the things we fear are going to make us suffer or hurt us, what is even scarier is the fact that something might **take away our happiness.**

Imagine yourself waiting for the weekend to roll around for the past five days. But suddenly, you manager informs you that there will be overtime work on Saturday because of a glitch in the computers, and the work is due by Monday. Even if you're told this is more of a "request for a favor," as a good employee, you'll probably say "Yes." But unhappiness will arise in that instant.

If presented with the possibility of increased suffering in the future, we will feel worse just thinking about it, especially when we perceive that our happiness is being taken away.

What we desire is certain future happiness. But in reality, **it's impossible to be lucky all the time.** Suffering is a part of life. Suddenly, the happiness we were expecting might vanish before our eyes.

At the beginning of this section, I mentioned how our peak happiness occurs right before we get what we want. But at the same time, the moment we suffer the most is the second we anticipate the suffering itself or before our happiness gets taken away. If experiencing future happiness is considered a bonus, anticipating future suffering is a loss.

Instead of suffering once or for a short period of time when the cause of suffering actually arrives, we stretch out our own suffering. So what do we do with this type of suffering?

Let's Think of Something Else

Worry about the future causes us to suffer on account of things that don't yet exist. We might even miss a good opportunity to be happy because of something like that. This is equivalent to feeling pain before you are hit or burning before the flame touches your skin.

The suffering that you imagine will occur in the future is not happening yet. To look at it another way, if we were to stop thinking about it we could solve this type of suffering directly. If we don't pay it any attention, it can't really hurt us. We can't go back to the past, and by the same note we are also unable to travel into the future. Thus, staying in the present is the best strategy.

However, **trying not to think of something is quite difficult**, perhaps even impossible. If somebody tells you "Don't think about bears for five minutes," can you really do it? If you told yourself not to think of bears, images of bears would likely appear immediately in your head. The more you try not to think of something--not to think of all the work you have to do tomorrow, for instance--the more you will think about it.

A method of stopping yourself from ruminating about something is to **fill your head with other thoughts.**

Think about other things, especially things that better capture your attention. This works best if they are things that make you feel even better. However, even thoughts that cause a little bit of stress, if they can still make you feel better than thinking about your main anxiety, will be a small improvement. **As long as it's something that pulls your attention away,** it's enough. Also, it's much better to select thoughts you can think about for a while. For example, instead of worrying about your results on an entrance exam, you can think about the TV shows you saw last night, or even worry about that game level you couldn't clear for a long time, as long as it makes you feel better.

Thus, if ever you are plagued by worries of the future or have an undesirable event looming ahead, instead of telling yourself to forget it, it's better to distract yourself with something else.

For example, thinking about those TV shows. We might think back to the cliffhanger that left our female protagonist in a fight with her significant other and wonder whether the couple will get back together this time.

Alternatively, you can think about events in the past that make you happy. Think back to when you were on a trip with your best friends, when it happened and where you went. Go back to when you were starting the trip, when you started the car engine, up until the last places you visited. Try and recall everything: the smells, the tastes, the sights, and the conversation.

You can think about activities that require a lot of brain power or analysis. Is there a puzzle or problem you could be dissecting (that doesn't cause you stress)? You could sit and plan for something that interests you such as mapping out your dinner menus for the whole week or analyze the direction current events will take in your country.

If you are afraid that might get you more stressed out, you could think instead about a hobby of yours. Perhaps, gaming captures your interest. You can think of strategies which could lead to a better score. For those who play sports, you could think about ways to improve your technique or the logistics of scheduling a future practice. For those who make things with their hands, imagine a project you've always wanted to do—materials, colors, and design.

If you are free and don't have much to think about, you could consider spending time on a new hobby. Find a new project, sport, or craft that you want to try and learn it from scratch.

This method can help to alleviate suffering generated from future events and will also stop you from worrying about them so much.

To this point, I've been encouraging you not to think so much about the future. I do want to say, though, that if thinking about the future helps you to prepare for a better outcome and to avoid painful mistakes, then it's good to spend some time on it. However, don't overdo it. If you think you're prone to over planning to the extent that you start to feel bad, then it's better to avoid it or to do it for only a short time.

As for making preparations for the future such as taking health supplements before being exposed to stress or visiting the temple to pay respect to your ancestors or any other preparations before the event, it's great as long as it allows you to feel better without adding to your stress, for example, costing you more than you can afford.

Failing in the Past, as One May in the Future

The past not only bridges the present with one's memories, but it also connects us to the future.

If we made a mistake in a particular situation and in the future encounter a similar situation, anxieties and fears may plague us. We are afraid of making the same blunders and suffer because of this fear.

For example, a dance student was preparing for a test and had one move which she could never get right no matter how hard she tried. Her instructor told her it was still unacceptable and in need of improvement. She received a bad evaluation. When the time came for the final test, self-doubt plagued her, and she was even more worried about failing.

When we have a negative experience that causes us to feel bad or to suffer greatly, we naturally feel uncomfortable or fearful when we encounter similar situations.

A good illustration would be a wife who has to visit her parents-in-law. She knows they dislike her. The last time she went to see them, she had to sit by and listen to her mother-in-law insult her the whole time. Her father-in-law hardly spoke to her or gave her as much as a glance. She was really uncomfortable the whole time. When the time comes to visit them once more, the memories of that time cause her a lot of discomfort and suffering.

In this type of situation, we experience anxiety both about past and future events, which are connected. Even if we have not yet come across the situation itself and we don't know for sure how it'll turn out, we still imagine the worst. But because the future events have similar aspects to what we have once experienced, we remember our past suffering and become convinced that our experience will be repeated, causing us to suffer before that repeated event even takes place.

Even optimists may not be able to resist the temptation to assume the repeated even will turn out badly. When we judge our future according to probabilities, knowing the past allows us to estimate outcomes in the future.

We know the dance moves we have to practice, including the one we can't nail no matter what. So, in the next test we became sure that we will fail to do it properly.

We know that our in-laws hate us. So whenever we pay them a visit, we don't expect them to welcome us with open arms. Most likely, we will just have to push through it.

However, this doesn't always have to be so.

There Are Two Sides to the Future Coin

"Prediction is very difficult, especially if it's about the future."

Niels Bohr – Danish Physicist

First off, the thing we should understand is that the future isn't as predictable as we may believe. We may anticipate a certain event with absolute certainty, but in the end the outcome shows something entirely differrent.

This can be both a good and a bad thing. The bad thing is that we can't be 100% sure about anything. There are variables and risk factors in everything. However, the good thing is that **we don't have to fall absolutely**

into despair because there are chances things might not turn out the way we imagine.

Moreover, when predicting the future based on our past experiences, one thing that may be different from the past is ourselves. We may not be the same person we used to be yesterday. There may be problems we don't know how to solve, but little by little our way of seeing things and our ability to react to them undergoes change. Small as the changes may seem, they can cause a huge ripple in terms of our ability to respond to the events in our lives.

One analogy is learning to swim or ride a bicycle. For some beginners, they're hopeless that they'll ever learn properly, but then they are suddenly able to do it, while never noticing what has changed in themselves. It is an accumulation of changes that suddenly "click" into place or reaching the threshold of knowledge that allows the problem to be solved. However, most of us don't know where that threshold is. We have surely improved, but we don't have a gauge to know whether we are far or near to the effective point of change. Therefore, don't rush to underestimate your-selves and think that you can't do it, that it can't be solved, or that you'll certainly fail.

Sometimes, an action we take seems unrelated to solving our problem, but in fact, it is. Building on the previous example, if we got a bad score in the latest dance test and feel that the beat of the music is hard to follow, we can improve our ability to follow it by listening to it more often. Even if we believe that this factor is not exactly what brought on our instructor's criticism, just by being better able to detect that one beat, it might improve our performance tenfold.

If we are disliked by our in-laws, we might take more time to think about the appropriate clothing to wear. Even when we feel we are overthinking things, changing our style of dressing might play in our favor if the in-laws are quite traditional and conservative.

We can't do anything about past events, but future ones are a different story.

As we learn and grow, we know more. And even though that can't change everything that will happen in the future, it allows us to adapt and improve how we deal with things.

Thus, minor change is a great thing. If we fail at our task, we can figure out better way to do it. Who knows, maybe it will yield much better results.

Albert Einstein, the great physicist, once said, *"Insanity: doing the same thing over and over again and expecting different results."*

Whenever we arrive at the conclusion that, no matter what we do, the results will be the same, we will fall into despair, afraid because we believe we can't escape failure. **Trying making changes** isn't such a bad thing. At the very least, we have the chance of a different outcome. Although it's true that changes can also cause events to take a turn for the worse, it allows us to realize that we have the power to change.

As I have mentioned, it's always important that we learn our lessons and use our valuable, previous experiences to keep us from making the same mistakes. Or even if we make mistakes in the future, know that we can overcome them because of our past experiences. We are still standing after encountering all these events, so we won't have to fear future situations because we have learned from the past.

Remember to keep telling yourself that the future is not for certain, we can't say for sure that darkness awaits us, because there are silver linings in every cloud.

The Future and Destiny

"If we wait until our lives are free from sorrow or difficulty, then we wait forever. And miss the entire point."

Dirk Benedict- American actor

There probably isn't much better than knowing that our future has only happiness waiting for us.

However, in reality, that's impossible. Sooner or later, something will happen that tells us we might meet bad things in the future.

It's human nature to want to plan. But because there's no such thing as a perfect plan, we can't really control and anticipate every little detail of the future.

Things happen that we could never predict: these are what I call "fate." We have only a partial hand in what happens in the future; the rest lies at the mercy of events outside our control, whether caused by the actions of others or by nature itself.

For example, if we were fully prepared for the work presentation, made secondary plans for every aspect, but there happens to be a blackout on the presentation day and we didn't get the chance to present, or our boss was in a bad mood from arguing with his wife at home and felt displeased with our work. These are things out of our control. We can't really prevent a power outage or ensure good relations between our boss and his wife.

Things that are out of our hands aren't always a bad thing for us though. It may be turn out more positive than we would have thought. Using the same example, on the day of the presentation our boss might have gotten a promotion and be in a great mood, so he might find the presentation to be good. Or maybe we were running behind schedule and there happens to be a blackout. So we were given more time to prepare, ensuring a better presentation.

It's impossible to predict events like power outages or strife in the lives of those close to us, but they may substantially affect our lives. The world is complex, and people are connected in complex ways. There's no way we can truly see what will happen.

Nonetheless, not everything is out of our control. Because even when we can't direct everything the way we want it to be, we do have a choice in certain matters. Imagine a student who has never studied for a test before in his life compared to another student who put in a tremendous amount of effort and systematically reviewed for the test. With equally capable brains, the latter is more likely to get a better score.

In my country there is a famous slogan that says, "Accidents can be prevented if you're careful," which demonstrates the belief that it does make a great difference if you are careful in everyday life.

By planning ahead and preparing for the worst, we can deal with the future better. But know that things should be done in moderation. We can attempt to make the future as easy as possible by thinking over the options, having a plan B, or creating solutions to potential future problems. But take care not to overdo it. If sitting down and making these plans becomes an obsession that causes you anxiety, learn to stop and find something else to do or think about.

Another thing we must come to accept is that we can't be 100% sure of anything. Our lives will not follow the path we lay out so carefully all the time. But we can learn to deal with the negatives so that we decrease the negative impacts on ourselves. As mentioned, humans are more capable of dealing with problems than we would like to believe, and there are very few issues in this world that we can't deal with.

If we imagine ourselves as investors, no matter what type of investor and no matter how skilled, there are always risks of making a bad investment with little return. However, the investor continues to invest without ruminating over and over about the loss or trying to search for investments without any risks, which don't exist.

Our lives are the same. If we do our best today with our mental, emotional and physical resources, review our mistakes and try to improve ourselves, that is enough. Because there is no reason for us to lament over something that has yet to happen.

If you experience happiness through anticipating pleasant events, consider it a bonus. But if you anticipate a negative event that causes us sorrow in the present, leave it for the future you to deal with.

Chapter 3: The Present, the Body, and the Mind

"…When you're in sorrow, everything seems grim. Your body has no energy to even think about getting up. You want to lie there, perhaps, to sleep forever. There is no motivation to work or go anywhere. Not even to eat.

I want to live in this silence. Why can't I? I'm not in the mood to do anything else."

In the past two chapters, we talked at length about the two main types of suffering which are suffering caused by the past and suffering caused by the future. These two are often linked by thoughts, memories, and expectation.

When we speak of "the human mind," we typically mean our thinking and invisible thought mechanisms that may affect us.

Many of you may have heard that the "mind" and "body" are linked. If your heart is hurt, your body may also become sick and weakened. There are many diseases and ailments that are actually caused by suffering and sorrow. This is especially true for gastritis, insomnia, acid reflux, and heart diseases which are frequently caused by stress.

When our hearts (emotional state of being) are in a weak state, our immune system doesn't function properly. Thus, we are liable to become sick quite easily.

This is why, if we have already acknowledged the fact that our lives will always be plagued with suffering, sadness, and worries that can have a lasting impact on our heart and body, we should figure out ways to properly deal with this fact.

In previous chapters, I introduced methods of dealing with fearful thoughts and related mechanisms, from changing one's way of thinking to recalling positive memories or even diverting one's attention to something else. But if you feel like you need other strategies to cope with sadness and anxiety, let's touch on something that holds a lot of influence over our minds and souls, which is **our very own bodies.**

The mind affects the body. When we feel hurt mentally, our bodies will also receive physical blows. If our minds are well taken care of, our bodies will be healthy. (Even though suffering affects our physical body more than happiness, that does not mean happiness will not affect our bodies as well.) On the other hand, a sickly body can also negatively affect one's state of mind, while a healthy body will serve as a foundation for inner happiness.

Even if it's true that just because we are healthy we won't necessarily achieve happiness, we could say that health is the foundation for happiness. If we are unwell and suffering from diseases, it's difficult to feel happy.

In this third chapter, we will talk about the connections between our minds and bodies, in the hope that we can adjust our actions and behavior in order to increase our potential for happiness and find it easier to mitigate our sufferings.

Because the mind and many of our thought processes are hidden by mechanisms that we can't see, but our bodies are easily observable to us, this is why changes that affect our bodies in a good way will likely make us happier as well.

Let's delve into this topic in more detail.

The Tired Body Tires the Soul; the Sick Body Sickens the Soul

The first step of inviting happiness into our lives and kicking suffering out is to have a healthy body.

Whenever we are ill or sick, it's not surprising if this is one more thing that makes us unhappy. This sickness or bodily discomfort is one thing that causes suffering. Moreover, illness brings with it a much lower tolerance against other suffering.

Humans' level of tolerance is limited. Imagine if you were unwell. You not only have to withstand the discomfort while engaging in other tasks, but even simple things like going out to have a meal or accomplishing daily activities would feel like a much heavier load than usual. And think about how much worse it would feel if you had to face other things that cause you suffering, like taking an important test or meeting angry boss.

Imagine a housewife who diligently does all her chores without complaint even when she has to clean a dirty toilet. But one day she gets ill and still has to do all of the usual housework. Seeing the state of the toilet while she is suffering so terribly upsets her. Why is it that she has to clean this toilet every single day? How many times has she told her husband and children to keep it clean?

Or for example, we might have a friend who is on the heavier side who has never cared about how his friends teased him about it, even when they called him "Piggy." However if he gets sick one day, having to force himself to go to school is already difficult enough. When his friends start in on him again, it's too much for him to bear. They have no idea they're adding more to his plate than he can take. He snaps at them and takes his leave.

Despite how obstacles such as getting sick are a normal part of our lives, **our bodies regularly have a mechanism name "self-control"[5] which withstands all kind of adversities in life.** You can think it as our tolerance as fuel in a tank. As we have to deal with obstacles, the fuel slowly empties. While it's true that it naturally constantly gets refilled, certain things like getting sick can cause the fuel in our tank to be used at a faster rate, which causes us to have lower tolerance for other things.

Similar to the above examples, there is a phenomenon known as "getting hungry." When our body feels hungry, we may be

---

[5] Gailliot, M. T., Baumeister, R. F., DeWall, C. N., Maner, J. K., Plant, E. A., Tice, D. M., ... & Schmeichel, B. J. (2007). Self-control relies on glucose as a limited energy source: willpower is more than a metaphor. *Journal of personality and social psychology, 92(2)*, 325.

quicker to anger. Even with something that annoys us a little may be enough to trigger that feeling of irrationality.

The blood sugar level, aside from its correlation to our physical strength, can also affect our tolerance. This is why we should not allow ourselves to be so hungry especially when trying to lose weight. Because it will make you feel worse about other activities (but overeating can also cause many ailments, so moderation is key).

Thus, whenever you are facing stresses in life and realize that you haven't been taking care of your body, even if you don't feel like it, remember to force yourself **and get into a habit of exercising, eating good food, and getting enough rest.** As these things have an impact on your emotions, you will find they do affect your ability to deal with adversity.

In troubling times, humans may find they lack motivation to do anything. Even someone who keeps an active lifestyle may find it hard to get up for a walk. Someone who loves to eat might lose their appetite. Although it's not unusual to take a break from everything once it a while, we must not allow such breaks to negatively impact us.

Remember that physical and mental motivations often go hand-in-hand. We can't punch or kick at sorrow to pull ourselves out of it physically, but if we are physically strong, it can help us find the strength to overcome our mental suffering as well.

Having physical strength might not make our point of view more positive, but it allows us to have more energy to deal with all the sorrows, suffering, and sadness better. The mind and the body are connected. If we don't heal our mental wounds, at least we can try to fix our physical scars first.

Force a Smile to Smile For Real

*"We shall never know all the good that a
simple smile can do."*

Mother Teresa

Have you ever asked yourself, "What am I feeling right now?"

Typically we don't have to question whether we are feeling good or bad. We know when we're feeling good, and the same goes for negative feelings. Not much thought is put into finding out what it is you're feeling. The mind makes that calculation for us.

Regardless, this mechanism isn't always accurate. There may be times when feelings signal to us whether things that occur are reasonably good or bad, but not all of them are based on actual things that have occurred.

One thing that tells us we're either sad or happy will be **whether our behaviors are like those of someone who is glad or who is unhappy.**

This might not seem to make much sense. When we hug our knees and somebody tells us we shouldn't look so depressed despite our feeling completely fine, this subconscious external behavior signals to us our emotional state. There are many research papers that show the effect of smiling or frowning. For example, a study by Wollmer and his colleagues showed that participants who had been treated with Botox--the chemical that causes temporary paralysis in certain facial muscles, making frowning more difficult—tended less to become depressed.[6]

---

[6] Wollmer, M. A., de Boer, C., Kalak, N., Beck, J., Götz, T., Schmidt, T., ... & Sönmez, D. (2012). Facing depression with

Body and mind are connected. Some mental mechanisms that deal with happiness and sadness can also affect our physical body. When you smile brightly, it makes your brain think that you are feeling happy. But when your face shows sadness, your brain will assume you are sad.

Try this out yourself. When you're feeling neutral, stand in front of a mirror and make an irritated expression. You will find you're feeling a bit more unhappy than usual. But if you start smiling, you will start feeling a bit happier.

While the effect isn't big enough to make a difference with very strong emotions, for instance, forcing yourself to smile when you're very upset, it does allow you some control. "Behaviors reflecting happiness" like smiling, being energetic, or joyous make it easier for us to feel happy. "Behaviors that

botulinum toxin: a randomized controlled trial. *Journal of psychiatric research, 46(5)*, 574-581.

reflect sorrow" such as frowning, hunching over, and being lethargic makes us more prone to feeling sad.

This is why, if someone tells you to smile more when you're sad, it's a good first step. Even if the effects aren't immediate, smiling more will allow us to be happier later. On the other hand, try not to act like a person who is suffering, because it will make you sadder in the long run.

So keep acting like you're happy, smile and be energetic, because you can trick your brain into thinking you are happy with relatively little effort.

Aside from a healthy body serving as the foundation of a happy mind, a body expressing signs of happiness will provide the same effect as well.

Do Nothing-Yet

This topic is not related to alleviating suffering but is a warning as to how present suffering may cause further suffering in the future.

In the heat of moment, whether you are feeling extreme sadness or even happiness, it may not be the most appropriate time to make an important decision.

While it's also true that we don't always use reason in every decision even in a normal state of mind – occasionally doing things on a whim such as going shopping, eating sweets, or having a drink--but they are often small and have minuscule effects and often do not require a lot of self-control to pull back from.

However, during times of intense emotion we should refrain from making decisions that will impact our future or affect an area of life that holds great importance for us.

In a lover's quarrel, both sides may be feeling very angry or hurt, and this emotional state greatly impacts decision-making. Break-ups that occur in such moments are subject to regrets later on by both parties. This type of decision is one that will have a substantial effect on a person's emotional being in the future.

Or when an employee who has argued with their manager or colleague decides to quit when they are feeling irate and upset, they might realize later that they have made a huge mistake that will have a major impact on their life.

Although wrong decisions are normal, regardless of whether they are based on emotion or reason, allowing angry or depressed feelings to drive our decisions isn't the best idea even if it seems to make sense at the time.

Admittedly, although some may feel like they use more of their intuition and feelings, we are generally creatures of reason. In the background, we often weigh the pros and cons even if we are quite emotional at the forefront. Even more so when we look back at the past, we often evaluate the quality of our decisions. For example, we easily regret buying something when we don't use it at all-- perhaps we didn't think enough when we were purchasing it.

In the heat of the moment, we select options that appear to be the best at the time. Maybe it's better to part ways instead of arguing with your lover. Maybe it's easier to withdraw from a class if you dislike the lecturer. We may be controlled by our feelings and **nothing else makes more sense than our emotional state.**

But the problem is after our anger, hurt, and sorrow starts to evaporate, our reason kicks in.

A breakup may have seemed like the best solution, but once anger dissipates, the cons might actually outweigh the pros. Your significant other may be the most loving person despite your arguments. So why is it that you're now single and alone?

While under the sting of a rebuke, we might have thought our managers were evil and harsh, so much so that it's better to resign. But after some time, we may find that getting a job is extremely difficult and that manager will move to another department next year. We might questions ourselves as to why we quit despite the high pay.

Once we return to a neutral state, our choices may change **because during intense emotions in the moment, our reasoning functions differently.**

Basing decisions upon emotions might not always yield an incorrect result, but will our neutral self really agree with those decisions? Moreover, some choices can't be taken back.

Thus, in moments of high suffering and when we are emotionally wounded, it's better to avoid making important decisions (except in case of an emergency). Stop yourself, no matter how good your reasoning may seem at the moment, because when you return to normal, you may start seeing hidden faults in your decision-making process.

Always tell **yourself if it's a really good decision, if we think the same way after some time has passed, then it would be all right for us to wait before making the decision.**

This advice goes not only for negative extremes of emotion, but also for positive extremes as well. In the case of winning the lottery, intense elation may cause an individual to splurge and make unnecessary purchases. It's only after the feeling has passed and their joy subsides that they realize how much money they have wasted.

Remember **emotions are always fleeting but the consequences of our actions are permanent and often unchangeable.** Unless it's necessary to decide right away, take some time off before you do.

Face It Together, Walk Away If Necessary

It is good to be determined to face problems head-on. If we only run away from our problems, they will never be solved. On the other hand, this doesn't mean we have to deal with every single problem right away.

In the past two chapters, we talked of the causes for present suffering which are memories of the past and worries of the future. In truth, without these thoughts in our heads, we probably would not have to suffer in that moment.

We can escape for a time from our memories and sad thoughts. In a day, there's so much we have to do. Sometimes, we can forget things that cause us suffering for a while. But when we come across something that reminds us of a sad thought or stressful memory, the suffering will come back to visit us.

Fresh after a breakup, discovery of sentimental objects, previously-visited spots, favorite songs, or even your lover's favorite dishes will cause old memories to resurface. Every time you encounter them, they cause you sadness.

Or we might be stressing over an important presentation for school or work next month. After fully preparing ourselves we might still feel frazzled. Or maybe we might not think about it much until we open our laptops and see the presentation file that triggers the anxiety.

An easy way to look at this is the phrase "Out of sight, out of mind." If you don't encounter reminders of sad situations you won't think so much about them.

Just as it's hard not to think about a bear once it's entered our mind, putting a stop to our thoughts isn't very easy, but we can make our feet walk away from situations that cause us stress and use our two hands to help us set them aside so that the triggers are far away from where we are.

If a place makes us sad, we can try to avoid it to alleviate unnecessary suffering.

It's up to us whether we throw out the sentimental objects or shove them into the back of a drawer (to avoid the regret of throwing them away) as long as we don't have to see them with any frequency.

Many of us may begin to wonder if this isn't the same thing as avoiding our problems. Even though it's true that if we avoid a problem, we might have to avoid it forever, but as I have said before there is a difference between suffering caused by the past and suffering caused by the future.

Avoiding triggers of anxiety can be thought of as **not engaging in unnecessary problems.** Things we are worried about are the same ones that will happen no matter what, like worrying over a test. Whether we worry or not, once it comes we still have to take the test. Our job currently is to prepare for it the best we can and once we are ready, there's no use in mulling it over, stressing and suffering.

Thus, save future events for the future. If you're adequately prepared, the only thing left is for the time to come. There's no need to stress about it and rob yourself of present happiness.

As for avoiding things that have caused you suffering in the past, consider it **stepping back.** Obviously, I don't endorse this strategy forever. If you've broken up with an ex, it wouldn't be reasonable to never go back to places you had enjoyed with them. Problems of the past are passed and gone. We can't change that.

Still, taking a step back when you're not ready to deal with your problems isn't a bad thing. There's no use in forcing yourself to do something that causes you to suffer soon after experiencing a loss or major disruption. **Having to face a fresh issue is like slicing a new wound.** There's just no use if you're not ready.

In the chapter regarding the past, we talked about how, as time passes, issues that were once a huge problem will come to seem smaller. Something that was difficult to even think about at first would become easier to ponder as time passes.

Thus, if we're not ready, we don't have to face things that will "reopen our wounds" just yet. Stay away for now and when the time comes, the places that once caused us pain will slowly become just a typical place we're not attached to. While the connection with the hurt might not disappear completely, it will be so insignificant that we can cope with it.

In summary, it is okay to avoid situations that make us suffer as long as we don't keep it up forever. It's okay to take some time off until we feel ready to face our pain.

Nonetheless, **certain types of avoidance can give rise to more problems.** For example, our workplace might cause us suffering because we were chided by our supervisor, but we can't exactly stop going to work. (However, it might improve our outlook to take leave for a day or two—moderation is the key).

Aside from this, not everything is avoidable. There may be roads leading back to your house that reminds you of your ex. We can't avoid it. In these cases, we can only accept the situation and face it head on with the aforementioned techniques and strategies.

Search for Happy Memories

"Illusory joy is often worth more than genuine sorrow."

René Descartes – French philosopher
and mathematician

Aside from avoiding things that cause us pain, we can walk towards what gives us happiness.

When you're suffering and you have things you can do that bring you joy, even if it's something small (as long as it doesn't relate to the cause of your suffering where it can become a point for comparison), pick it up.

It may be a game, novel, cartoon, or movie you particularly enjoy which can bring a smile to your face—keeping in mind that if your issue is a broken heart, romance books or films may not be appropriate. Of course, there're no hard rules about this, as long as you're sure your activity won't negatively affect you.

Things that may give you happiness include not just physical objects, but can also be places. Some of us may have places that help us relax and feel peaceful or cheerful. Many love the beach, nature hikes, or visiting places of worship. Others, still, might enjoy the mall, cafes, and the busy life of a city. Those locations need not be travel destinations but any area that provides tranquility to the individual. However, it shouldn't be connected to your current suffering because your goal is to get away from all that for a while. Only after you feel more recharged should you go back to such places to recall the good memories.

If the weekend isn't long enough to visit your favorite place, taking a holiday leave might not be such a bad idea. A little time off can heal a wounded heart, so this may help you feel more rested and energized later on.

Not only do these little rays of happiness come in the form of objects or places, but activities can bring you joy. You may love playing the guitar, making music, dancing, doing woodwork, crafting, gardening or any other type of activity. Any of them can help.

For some people who are suffering, they may not want to do anything and instead prefer to sit around daydreaming or lamenting about life forever. Some problems may be too difficult to think about or find solutions for. Thus, it's not always beneficial to wallow in issues we can't control.

Moreover, many tend to overlook the little rays of sunshine in their lives. When one is plagued with worries for the future or the regrets of the past, it's common to forgo present happiness. Although if you're unhappy, it's not easy to "be motivated" to do much, training yourself to overcome that hurdle and appreciating the little things can yield great benefits in terms of relief of suffering.

Before doing those things you might question "How much will this help me?" or even after you do it you might feel "it's nothing special" but in the long run **happiness is similar to suffering, in that it slowly collects until it can affect us.** It may be harder to build a "happiness collection" than a "pain collection," but keep at it, and gradually you'll see what happens.

If you're still emotionally weak and not ready to let go of the sorrow, follow your heart. However, please remember that your body can make your mind better too, sometimes to a greater, sometimes to a lesser extent, so try to find something that will make you just a little bit happy. The benefits will definitely show in the end.

Don't Throw Everything Away

Franz Schubert – Austrian composer

It's in our nature to focus on suffering and to give a lot of weight to negative events because, as I've said before, it's evolutionarily beneficial to be wary of things that may cause us harm.

Nonetheless, there are few things in the present day that are truly dangerous. But because we were designed this way, or rather, evolved this way, no matter what type of suffering it is, we are especially receptive.

Any suffering still has the potential to interfere with our daily routines.

A common example would be a student going through heartbreak. For a teenager, there may be nothing more painful than a breakup. Many aspects of their lives are negatively impacted. They may lose all motivation and let go of their studies, daily activities, hobbies, and even the people around them to the point of losing their social lives and becoming reclusive.

This applies not only to youngsters but to adults as well. When anyone encounters an extremely negative event, be it heartbreak or other types of loss, the effects are the same.

At times, unexpected troubles may come our way. A family member may fall terminally ill or our spouse might part ways with us forever. When facing such a difficult situation, it's so hard to live your life as you normally would. You would want to stay home from work, forget to take care of your body, and leave your friends behind.

While it may sound harsh, one topic we should always keep in mind is other people. They may understand what we're going through, but there's only so much a person is willing to take. There's a limit for everyone.

Imagine is person suffering from a breakup. During that phase, enthusiasm for going to class, doing group work, and other tasks is non-existent. Friends may sympathize and attempt to help out, but they can't take that hurt away. The professors must also evaluate you by the same standards as everyone else. If the pain really has a huge impact on the student's studies and they fail a test that could be like rubbing salt in their wound.

Worse yet if it's your job we're talking about. Your colleagues and managers may empathize but the work still carries on. Even if you're not under threat of dismissal, not doing your job well can lower your chance for promotions or salary increases in the future.

Something most may forget while they are in pain is family. Many may withdraw into their own world to lick their wounds and may react badly when somebody comes along trying to help or asking about their situation. They may push the person way, hurting that individual in the process and negatively impacting their relations in the future. Everyone has their own emotions and experiences, so despite knowing how the other party is suffering, it may be hard to make allowances for unusual behavior.

Even though we may be particularly unmotivated to do anything else when we're suffering, **we still have to push ourselves to**. While doing those tasks might not help us feel better, say when we are hurt over family matters, going off to work is necessary even if it is physically tiring and mentally taxing. In fact, some people find that they feel better when they go to work for many reasons. For the example, they focus on the work rather than on their sadness, or a success at work might raise their awareness of the many things in life that make them happy. The problem is the taking that first step to decide to do something else. When you can take the first step, the second step will be easier, and so on.

If we are suffering at present, it doesn't mean our future has to be dragged down as well. The effort you put into work or relationships today is an investment in a (happier) future. You might not be able to reap the profits of your hard work today, but it may be an obligation too heavy to simply cast aside. You may be sad, in pain, stressed out, or depressed for whatever reason but you must work hard to protect the other aspects of your life.

In a way, life is similar to a TV drama. There may be filler episodes that you don't particularly want to watch or live through, but you still have to follow along the script and carry on acting. A common phrase known in the show business is "The show must go on," and that can apply to life as well, so no matter what, you still have to continue with your part.

Push yourself and grit your teeth a bit. When the sad spell passes, you will have a much brighter future or at least one that reaps the benefits of your own present efforts.

The Time Will Come When You're Ready

Emotions and thoughts are so intricately connected. Thus, altering our own emotions can be achieved by first changing our way of thinking. As many theories posit, in particular the cognitive approach, if we don't frame something as suffering, suffering will not occur.

Regardless, changing our thinking and perspectives toward situations and things is difficult. It's not as though we can simply tell ourselves to stop suffering, is it? If we are being burned by fire, telling ourselves it is not hot is futile. (At least not for typical humans. I still have yet to confirm the use of hypnosis in suppressing pain when walking across fires and such). In the same way, if triggers of suffering are present, no matter what we think, we probably still have to suffer.

However, this doesn't mean that we can't do anything. But what I want to say is it's not a matter of simply telling yourself "not to think" about it because that's nearly impossible.

Self-consoling and holding good memories close in order to redirect your attention, something I mentioned in previous sections, aren't difficult techniques you can follow to deal with immediate problems.

Still, in the long run, acceptance and a realistic life perspective--trying to see the silver lining in things--are the most important steps in dealing with serious issues.

While it's true that worries regarding problems of the future will dissipate once the situation arrives, similar situations will still invoke the same feeling and suffering every time if you don't learn to cope with worry.

Regarding issues of the past, while we might not be able to forget every little detail of our experiences, we can still let go of some of them. If you let some part of them go, the rest of them will be easier to forget. This proves that time is a friend to change. In the future, when we encounter events that make us suffer, we can be sure that time will help us the same way.

Humans constantly grow every day. I believe even without reading this book or ever reading books about dealing with suffering, the gained life experience you gain will likely teach you to be strong bit by bit. People who have faced a lot of terrible situations in life who have now healed from them often have the strongest minds. In many cases, however, suffering lasts for a very long time and affects the individual's life too much. Sometimes, we want a "tool" or "helper," and so getting help from someone like a counselor or reading self-help books may allow suffering individuals to recover much faster.

Resilience in the face of suffering is something that happens naturally over time. As we travel through life, there are tips and techniques we will pick up along the way. This will make our journey much easier.

In the coming pages, we will be talking about techniques that will help us deal with our emotions in the present to mitigate their impact as much as possible. Because thinking alone doesn't always do the trick, these are other strategies that we can utilize to help ourselves.

Rehearse in Writing

*"I write to understand as much as to be
understood."*

Elie Wiesel – Jewish American writer
and political activist

The fact that our thoughts, feelings, and emotions are unobservable inside our head can be the root of many problems. The first is they aren't fully controllable. We cannot repress, alter, or change internal things that easily. The second issue is that we don't really know what the underlying mechanisms are.

Have you ever tried to change your thoughts and realize that no matter how much you try, it seems like nothing is improving? Let's illustrate with an example.

One couple argues every single day. The girl cries herself to sleep every night. The guy also feels a similar kind of pain. But because they believe in their love, they stick with the relationship for a long time. However, with the passage of time, the tolerance of each is depleted until both decide to part ways.

Even if the decision came about from both parties, it's still difficult see it as a positive change, and it will be hard not to feel down in the dumps after such a breakup.

The lady has it worse than the man. At first, she feels the wave of depression hitting her and feels that life sucks. Whenever she feels that way, she rationalizes to herself that she did the right thing and that it was the best for both of them. However, no matter how reasonable the decision was, she still feels as bad as ever.

Sometimes even if the decision was reasonable and the choice was correct, emotions can still be tumultuous.

Thoughts and evaluations of past events affect our emotions. On the flip side, emotions can also affect thoughts and judgments. Emotions and thoughts both reside in our heads. When we attempt to block out emotion, we're bound to meet with adversity at every turn.

Thus, instead of letting negative thoughts play with our hearts and minds, let's find something to pull those negativities into something tangible, something we can physically see.

One easy way that works is jotting down your feelings of the moment on a piece of paper or, if you're a more tech-savvy person, typing it works as well (whether it's on your phone, tablet, or computer, anything will work, as long as it's written down tangibly).

Many of you might be curious as to how writing things down will help.

Sometimes when we try to work out a problem in our minds, our thinking becomes unclear, disorganized or muddled. The more complex the thing we're thinking about, the harder it is to see the big picture. For the example, you may not be able to mentally arrange your monthly schedule or solve a complicated math equation in your head and may require pencil and paper to work it all out.

Feelings work similarly. Writing down our emotions will allow you to experience them more tangibly. You thoughts will be **more coherent** as well because thoughts in our head are ever-changing. When we think about something new, especially if the new thought is emotionally-laden, the old thought might get pushed out and forgotten. But by writing it down, you can see it, reread it, and understand it better.

"...I know that everything I did was because of things that happened in the past. I

didn't break up with him because of my emotions, and it wasn't something that happened out of the blue. Both he and I hurt each other whenever we're near each other. Despite our best efforts, we can't seem to meet halfway. We've been suffocated and hurt long enough.

While I may be lonely and depressed, if I really think about it, this is probably better than tolerating our incompatibility, having to argue and hurt each other's feelings."

You need not write out a novel or describe things eloquently. There's no need for fancy quotes, so long as you write what you think. And when you are done, **try reading it over** and you might notice that what you have written describes the very reasons for your actions.

Another benefit of putting thoughts onto a paper is that you are forced to **arrange the thoughts** inside your brain in a way that makes them more coherent and allows you to understand yourself better.

On many occasions, you might feel that you fully comprehend your own thoughts and feelings of the moment, but you might find that it is more difficult than you'd thought to form them into a story line. The tangled web of ideas and emotions can make it complicated to differentiate clearly between heads and tails.

Being able to think over your own thoughts will allow you to ensure that your reasons for your actions are sound, so that you don't need to worry, feel guilty, or criticize your actions.

"…I have prepared myself the best I can. I don't have to worry about next week's task…"

"…I've done my best in the past. I shouldn't have to blame myself for the breakup…"

"…Everyone gets sick and is hospitalized at some point. There's probably a bunch of other people who have the same sickness as me. I shouldn't worry so much about the treatment…"

"…At that time, I really had no idea he felt that way, that's why I said what I did. I don't need to keep blaming myself…"

Believe it or not, there is a huge difference between thinking inside your head and writing thoughts down. **The thoughts running over and over in your mind aren't as convincing to yourself as putting them down on paper or the computer screen.**

If you write down your thoughts and feelings, you might learn that you are able to discover more about yourself.

Talk about Your Suffering to Change Your Thoughts

If you're someone with baggage, when you go to meet others, whether friends, parents, or siblings, they all are willing to listen to your troubles. This is a good thing. Getting to vent about your feelings through talking with someone can help lighten your load.

In truth, getting to talk about our problems can be useful in that the listener might have good suggestions we can follow. But if it's your very own problem, shouldn't you know the details best and have the most understanding of how to best resolve it? What are the benefits of talking about our troubles to others?

If you've ever had someone vent to you, you may realize that you can be a pretty effective listener. When someone asks you for advice, good ideas flow out smoothly, **but when you have that same problem yourself, why is it so difficult to solve?**

For the most part, it's not as though we have no solutions to our own issues. Sometime, we might even know well enough what the most appropriate course of action is.

If we were dumped, we know we should move on. Thinking about the old days will only bring pain, and imagining what he could be doing is not good for us.

If we worry about work, we know it's best to prepare well and that it's useless to worry so much about the future.

If we made a mistake, we know to forgive ourselves. And, if there's no way to fix the error, then we must use the past as a lesson without needlessly stressing over it.

But as with the topic of the previous section, if we only think to ourselves, we often have to constantly battle the thoughts alone.

More often than not, we will lose to emotions. This is why trying to change the perspective of the bad event by ourselves is often not effective.

In truth, venting and conversing about your emotions to close others employs a similar technique to writing them down on paper. Telling someone else about our feelings allows us to better form our internal state into something coherent in order to make the person understand. This is equivalent **to organizing your own thoughts for yourself.**

Having an individual listen to us and having them concur with our thoughts is better than sitting around and pondering alone. Instead of thinking about changing our thoughts and negative emotions, speaking lets us clarify our thoughts. Better yet, it can increase our confidence in our conclusions if the other party supports them.

Sometimes, venting doesn't even require the person in question to say anything. Just getting the opportunity to speak may be enough. When we are suffering or are plagued by issues, if they are our own problems we often know best about what we should do, the only hindrance being our tumultuous emotions getting in the way of reasonable thought. **Getting to organize our thoughts, saying them out loud, and having a listener will make us form our ideas more tangibly.** When we externalize our thoughts, they are less likely to get blown away by our emotions.

While it's true that telling people your thoughts isn't always enough to add weight to your reasoning or to change how you think immediately, it is often better than ruminating alone.

This technique not only allows you to release the pent up emotions, but we can also learn how to effectively deal with others when they wish to vent to us as well.

The Event, the Reasoning, and the Emotions

As I review the research literature, no matter what techniques or theories are proposed to lessen suffering, the basic idea is the same. **We must begin by understanding that emotion itself before anything else.**

Emotions are things that occur without our conscious control. When we encounter a situation, we unconsciously react to it. We may wonder why we suffer because of certain events and why it's natural to feel sad with events such as a great loss, running into obstacles in personal or work life, or encountering things we dislike. The big question remains **why do we have to suffer in these types of situations?**

Many of you might be thinking, what's the use of knowing the answer to that?

If something bad happens and we feel bad about it, isn't that just natural?

But what I want to get across is that there isn't always a clear cause for our emotions. Our bodies may seem to have an automated system that tells us what to feel, but we aren't enslaved to our own emotionality. **We are often governed by reason and often refuse to believe things that don't make logical sense.** This is why we shouldn't just go along with our automatic feeling especially if it is one of sorrow and suffering.

The founding philosophy of religions such as Zen Buddhism teaches us to examine our own suffering until we understand it well. Doing so will allow us to realize that the situation is quite normal and that we don't even need to suffer over it. It's simply a part of life.

Regardless, this book isn't here to merely tell you to look at things more carefully in order to eradicate all suffering. As with everything, practice makes perfect and practice takes time. However, by putting in more effort you will soon realize that you are causing yourself too much unwarranted suffering.

In certain circumstances, suffering settles in our heart **because we are used to it or we are taught** from a young age that if something negative happens, it must be like the end of the world. But in all honesty, by examining the situation carefully, we will learn that it doesn't have that much of an effect on us. Moreover, there isn't a need to suffer so much. In some cases, we **might have already overcome the same obstacle in the past multiple times** without costing us our arms and legs in the process.

A good example is when a couple argues and the man always refuses to talk to the woman for some days, during that period, the woman might feel down and unable to eat or sleep because she has learned this behavior from others around her. This behavior typifies a view that can be stated as "If your boyfriend completely stops talking to you, that's something extremely horrendous!" But if she takes a closer look, she might realize that it was simply how her boyfriend has always acted every time they argued. After a few days, he'll turn back to normal, and all she had to do was wait for a while.

Another issue is when we allow automated feelings to govern ourselves. When we are in pain, we often think only of negative events and that, in turn, makes us feel even worse. But if we look carefully, we will be able to pick out the good **things or at least know that there is always hope and there's no need to see everything so negatively.**

For example, a teenager might get into the last university of his choice, one in a much smaller city, which is in no way comparable to the prestigious colleges in the city where he lives. At that moment, he might feel great suffering because he has always been told that if he wanted a better future, he must attend one of the big universities located in his city. However, if he actually thinks about it, his dorm that is so far away from home could offer him the type of freedom he has always wished for. On the other hand, if he had lived in the city, he might need to stay home, encounter a lot of traffic, and be stuck with the old way of living. While he may be disappointed in the university he is in, there are always hidden silver linings in everything.

Despite the fact that using reason and seeing things objectively might not always clear all our feelings of suffering or even change them into something more positive, at the very least we will be able to find some positive aspects of our situation, find solutions to our problems, or mitigate the blow of whatever issue we are dealing with. We don't always have to see everything objectively but if the situation is causing us to suffer, we might need to take a closer look at it to see the cause-and-effect patterns and reasons why we are suffering. We'll learn if it is actually worth our suffering.

If the picture never gets clearer no matter how we look, no matter what viewpoint we take, and we can't find the positives in the big picture, we can use some of the previously described techniques to aid the process. Writing or talking to someone else allows us to form our thoughts about the situation regardless of whether we write them down with pen and paper, on a computer, or speak of them to close others: it allows us to see things more clearly.

Bad things may happen to us, and as humans we will suffer, but these are ways to limit our suffering and preventing needless pain. Our emotions might lead us to feel great suffering when we are faced with situations that may be bad for us even when we don't need to suffer. Thus, by taking an in-depth look into things and finding different perspectives, we will find ourselves suffering less.

What We Want and What We Are Capable Of

"We do not succeed in changing things
according to our desire,
but gradually our desire changes."

Marcel Proust – French novelist

In times of trouble, if there were a way to be free of suffering most people would use it. Especially if it is something that makes you suffer a lot, no matter how hard that task is, you would likely try to achieve it.

While putting in your best effort is a good thing, and we are told from a young age that "Where there's a will, there's a way," you have to make sure it's the right type of effort.

For example, we might want to get a high grade on a test and instead of taking time for reading, we go to a temple to pray even if the temple is one that's extremely far away in a provincial area. Doing all that instead of reviewing for your test may be considered a type of effort but one that is futile in producing the result we want.

Many attempts to escape from suffering fall into a similar category. Some people tend to think that if we are suffering, we can't just sit still and just let it happen to us. Isn't it much better to get up and do something? Won't it be better to try every way possible to stave off this bad experience? But as they say, there are ways and ways. Some ways are more effective than others.

If there were set ways of avoiding suffering, as simple as earning more money by working more hours, all the diligent people in this world wouldn't be in so much pain. But life just doesn't work that way. There's no set method for dealing with suffering, because it comes in so many different shapes and forms.

However, this doesn't mean that we can't do anything to deal with our suffering. Otherwise, this book wouldn't have been written in the first place. But the techniques we have gone through earlier can't completely rid us of suffering.

Great sufferings often take a long period of time to deal with. Irrespective of how hard you try or how many techniques you utilize and self-help books you read, it won't guarantee a quick end to suffering.

This is like trying to cure a disease. Time is an important component to healing. Taking two times your recommended dosage won't help you heal faster. Having a beneficial surgery over and over will not help the patient but would lengthen their recovery time and put them in danger. Time has a huge role to play in healing.

However, each and every one of us is different. Some heal faster, others gradually.

But given the right treatments both can recover over time.

Thus, **what we should be doing is what isn't too hard to do right now.** You don't have to force yourself to succeed immediately. There are ways you can manage and gradually change the way you think. As time passes, that suffering will also disappear --no longer present to disrupt our relationships and other aspects of life.

Even during times they're not suffering, some people might still try all sorts of methods and tricks to ward off suffering and put their minds at ease. Some might have a "lucky object" they carry around or use during a crucial event, like a "lucky pen" for a test-taker; others might get involved in elaborate and expensive rituals they have been told will eliminate and mitigate their problems. But whatever it is you might wish to engage in, so long as you have the time or money, there is nothing wrong with these actions. Just don't become so obsessed that your studies, career, or family time gets affected. As always, pursue things in moderation.

In the midst of suffering, some turn to alcohol or cigarettes which are things I do not recommend. While a little on the occasion is all right as long as you don't drink excessively, these things are quick fixes and don't do anything to address our human conundrum. Moreover, these and other addictive substances are often more trouble than they're worth. I still have yet to meet anyone who can fully escape suffering from using these substances, particularly ones that are illegal, and it's more likely to add suffering on top of what you have now.

Despite eradication of suffering being something everybody seeks, remember to take a look at how you deal with suffering. Is it really something that will allow you to be free of the pain? Will it bring about other bad consequences later on? It's advisable to stay away from the aforementioned methods because, in addition to the reasons already stated, sometimes just doing nothing and waiting is the best way of dealing with your troubles.

Learning to refrain from reckless decision-making when you're in pain is a good skill to have to prevent yourself from doing things on a whim.

At this point, we have gone through all of the items in our first-aid kit. While I can't guarantee that my methods are superior to those of others, I can tell you that they are quite simple and not too hard to follow no matter what state of mind you're in, and they are certainly effective. I want this book to be like a first-aid box for your soul, aiming to patch up minor scrapes and wounds as the first line of defense for major pain and suffering. If we are able to deal with suffering the minute it occurs, we will be left with less of an emotional scar in the long run.

When we have a bit of happiness thrown into the mix, we typically suffer a little less. Additionally, it can even draw in more happiness and, in return, mitigate even more of our current suffering. Wounds can heal quickly, and despite some scarring, they won't hurt as much as when it there is a fresh injury. Who knows, we might even forgot about them completely.

As an afterword I would like to share with you a thought about suffering. Think of it as parting words before you finish this book.

Afterword

"Life is a ladder of individuals and natural changes. Do not force it because it will cause sorrow. Allow reality to be. Allow everything to flow along with the rhythm as it is supposed to."

Lao Tzu – Chinese philosopher

From a young age, we are taught that encountering events which cause us suffering is due to "bad luck." When we go through our life, we might think that if we weren't such an unlucky person, we probably wouldn't suffer so much or make so many mistakes. Our lives would likely be smooth sailing, perhaps not with extremely joyous moments but also without the terrible ones.

In reality, the picture-perfect life doesn't exist. Humans are humans. We are emotional creatures. So long as we are able to be happy, we are able to feel sad. As long as there is suffering, there is happiness. As a typical Homo sapiens in pursuit of happiness, we will find that the good and bad often come together.

Readers who have heard teachings of Buddhism may know that the ultimate goal is to reach Nirvana where neither happiness nor sorrow exists. To never suffer is to achieve that goal. But that's not what this book is aiming for. The author himself is but a man who is satisfied with the color mix of happiness and suffering.

If you are satisfied with happiness which results from acquiring desired possessions, meeting people to love, listening to a great tune, reading a good book, getting to travel, receiving a salary, getting to do things you like, and other sources of happiness whatever they may be; you must accept that this path will consist of both happiness and suffering. **There is no such thing as only having happiness.** In the same way, I believe, there is no path purely plagued by suffering. As for the question of other worlds or the afterlife, they may exist, but I'm not able to speak of that.

Acceptance is an integral part of life. Suffering is like a disease: there isn't a single person on earth who's never fallen ill. If we are able to accept the fact that we may suddenly fall ill sometimes, in the same way, we can accept the fact that suffering is like a sickness that will pass or at least be lessened. It's unlikely that it will kill you.

Encountering a negative experience in life, whether it's through our own actions or bad luck, doesn't always mean you have to feel suffering. At the same time, being in a positive situation doesn't necessarily lead to feelings of elation.

As touched upon at the beginning, happiness and suffering are open to individual interpretation. Similar situations might cause different degrees of happiness or sorrow. Thus, we can control how much we suffer through our outlook towards things that happen to us. Even if we may tend to see things in black and white, we can learn to see things as the lightest shade of gray possible.

If one day, we encounter a great suffering from the past or the future, the first thing we have to accept is that **this is normal.** When it does happen, know that there usually is a solution. But even there is none, there are always ways to lessen the blow. Although it may sound depressing the fact is that **happiness is fleeting** but, on the same note, there is always hope because **suffering doesn't last forever either.**

This book has reached its closing chapter. I hope that throughout this book, you have accumulated techniques on how to mitigate your own suffering and that you may find the strength to carry on to tomorrow. Humans are adaptive in the face of adversity and are more capable of dealing with suffering than most expect. I believe time is the best healing tool in this world. There's no suffering that we can't handle at all.

I wish you all hope in life. If you have hope, your life will always be filled with potential and opportunities to encounter both sad and happy adventures.

I humbly thank all that have taken part in the journey of this book with me.

www.ingramcontent.com/pod-product-compliance
Lightning Source LLC
Chambersburg PA
CBHW051257250726
48656CB00004B/1351